WINGS OF LOVE

A MEMOIR

BY NANCY RIVARD

WHAT THE WORLD'S MOST INSPIRING POLITICAL AND THOUGHT LEADERS SAY ABOUT WINGS OF LOVE...

"*Wings of Love* is a beautiful story written in a simple and riveting manner. Full of truths. Anyone that reads it will find inspiration either to start following his purpose or the energy to continue their path."

– *H.E. Mr. Nayib Bukele,* **President of El Salvador**

"*Wings of Love* is a truly courageous—even heroic—and heartwarming adventure to read and share widely! Having known Nancy from the time she began to manifest her vision for Airline Ambassadors International and following her trajectory with it closely all these years, I can vouch for this as a book no reader will be able to put down. It is sure to inspire you to roll up our sleeves and do our own parts in making our collective future the caring and sharing world of which we all dream."

– *Elisabet Sahtouris Ph.D.,* **Evolution Biologist and Futurist**

"*Wings of Love* by Nancy Rivard is not just a memoir; this is an inspirational adventure about one woman's journey into the multifaceted world of humanitarian work. Using the occupation of Flight Attendant, Nancy Rivard has accomplished her goal of helping people around the world to live a life of dignity and purpose. She is a two-time Nobel Peace Prize nominee."

– *Richard Jordan,* **Dean of United Nations Non-governmental Representatives**

"Nancy Rivard is one of those people that you meet and say to yourself, Thank God for her. Her undying support for those in need is unmatched only by her relentless willingness to help make a difference. There are numerous people who owe their lives to Nancy and her team—that is what I call a true hero. *Wings of Love* is the story of how one woman set about and succeeded in changing the world."

– *Marisol Nichols*, Actress

"Nancy Rivard is a beautiful woman, inside and out, who has led a beautiful life, *Wings of Love* invites the reader inside both the woman and her life."

– *Annette Lantos*, Chair Emerita of the Lantos Foundation for Human Rights & Justice

"If there was ever one who gave of herself, her support, her time and resources, it's Nancy Rivard. Side by side, she and her husband, David, turned Airline Ambassadors International into a platform to launch Survivor led organizations. I am forever grateful. I hope you love her story, *Wings of Love*, as much as I did."

– *Pastor Donna Hubbard*, Survivor of human trafficking

"Edmond Burke noted all it will take for evil to prevail is for good people to do nothing. Sometimes good people don't know what to do. Nancy and Airline Ambassadors are closing that gap. You will be inspired by her book, *Wings of Love*."

– *Hon. Chris Smith*, US Congressman, NJ

"*Wings of Love* is a world's precious masterpiece on the awakening path of humanity."

– *Tony and Tammi Le*, United Nations Peace Advocates

This book is dedicated to my father, *Theodore James Larson*. With his transition, he gave me the greatest gift of all: the adventure of finding my true purpose.

"A drop in the bucket is only a drop
A minor and moist detail,
One drop can't change the color or taste,
In a ten quart watering pail,
But if that drop has the color of Love,
And the taste of tears Divine,
One drop dropped into the vessel of Life,
Can change the water to wine."

My favorite poem, taught to me by Millard Fuller,
Founder of Habitat for Humanity.

CONTENTS

ACKNOWLEDGMENTS

I want to acknowledge professor Frank Chindamo, who originally inspired me to write a book on the story of Airline Ambassadors and has been an unfailing cheerleader for 20 years! Andreea Billig helped me actually write the book, and she has been the one person who really "got" what Airline Ambassadors was about. Without her support and beautiful heart, I could never have completed it. I also want to thank Kate Jewell and Mary Wotanis, who also helped with editing. I am very grateful to all my mentors and friends - many of whom wrote endorsements.

A special thanks to my wonderful husband, Dave, who has been my rock of support. To Chris Belknap, who helped me launch my vision, as well as Armando Bukele Kattan, who taught me about balancing power, humor, service and friendship.

Thank you for reading this book and bringing love into action every single day.

PROLOGUE

December 24, 1981

Daddy and Me, 1981

Christmas Eve always unfolded like a scene from a joyous Hallmark card in our La Jolla, home in Southern California. The festive spirit painted our surroundings with season decorations, stylish outfits, and radian smiles, creating a picturesque holiday atmosphere. The inviting aroma of freshly baked cookies and a sizzling roast emanated from the warm kitchen, enveloping the entire house in a tantalizing scent. Inside, Mother devoted hours to crafting culinary masterpieces with meticulous care.

My younger sister, Cheryl, and I enthusiastically adorned the Christmas tree, its branches stretching toward the ceiling, adorned with vibrant ornaments that sparkled in the light. The twinkling fairy lights bathed the room in a soft glow, while the scent of pine filled the air as we carefully placed the delicate glass baubles, their gentle clinks resonating the joy. Each ornament we hung filled us with the excitement of the holiday season, our fingers tingling with anticipation. We'd prepare cookies for Santa and joyfully sing along to Christmas carols.

Christmas Eve was also the one time of the year when the four of us went to church for midnight mass and joined our voices in song, like Silent Night, Hark the Herald Angels Sing or Joy to the World, which brought my dad immense joy to my dad, He cherished this festive tradition almost as much as when he and Mom would sneak into the living room early in the morning so he could snap a picture of us when we came into the room and saw Santa's bounty. However, that winter of 1981 painted a different picture. The perfect Hallmark card transformed into an unexpected black and white scene, tainted with the sterile scent of antiseptic. It began with an unforeseen call from Daddy during one of those typical winter afternoons in Southern California, featuring a pristine blue sky and delightfully mild sunshine. Freshly returned from a day at work as a supervisor for American Airlines flight attendants, I gazed out the window of my condo, captivated by the awe-inspiring ocean vista. My heart overflowed with elation, eagerly awaiting another enchanting Christmas with my loved ones. A graduate of the "charm farm" as they call the AA Flagship University, I was only 29, adored my job, had amazing prospects of climbing up the corporate ladder even higher, and was in love with a man that appeared to be my soul mate.

"Nancy, I need to go to the hospital," Daddy said right away. Although his voice sounded poised and fearless, as if he had just booked a routine check-up appointment, I immediately knew something was very wrong. Since I was a little girl, Daddy and I shared this special deep bond, which required no words. Six months before, doctors diagnosed him with inoperable bladder cancer, despite him never being sick a day in his life. To make matters even more dire, his body could not handle chemotherapy.

"But, Daddy, it's Christmas Eve! You can't go to the hospital," I protested, trying to contain the trembling of my voice and hoping my words would hold a magical power to delay the inevitable, perhaps curing him.

"I need to go, honey, to get some relief. Besides, those poor doctors could use someone like me to cheer them up!"

My darling Daddy! Even in the darkest hour, he put a smile on his face and mine. But it faded quickly, chased away by the knot in my throat. His sense of humor couldn't fool me—only a desperate situation would make him leave the home he cherished on Christmas Eve.

I hurried past the elegant dress I had planned to wear that evening, grabbed the handmade gift I had prepared for him, and hopped into my car, hoping for a smooth ride with empty roads and a string of green lights.

What if, what if…?

While my heart clung to hope, my mind painted a grim picture.

I couldn't bear the idea of Daddy going through any more suffering. I worshiped him and cherished our strong heart connection and refused to picture my life without it. Or him.

Daddy must have sent a guardian angel to watch over me, for I made it to the hospital in one piece despite the heavy, bitter tears clouding my vision.

When I pushed open the door of the hospital room, Daddy's head slightly turned toward it, as if he knew I was about to arrive. For a fleeting moment, his dim eyes livened up. I hugged Mother and Cheryl, then kissed his forehead—it was moist and warm—and sat by his side.

"Did you bring it?" my mother broke the silence after a short while.

I nodded and took Daddy's gift, wrapped in green and red shiny gift paper with a golden ribbon and bow, out of my suede briefcase. His lips curled into a little smile—this briefcase made him very proud of me. It was a self-made gift from a few years ago, symbolizing the celebration of my first major career milestone at American Airlines: the transition to flight attendant supervisor. The Christmas gift for Daddy—that one I had made it myself. It took me roughly a week to compile a picture book that chronicled the most blissful moments of our family life. Each picture, starting with Mother and Daddy's first dates up to the present day, was accompanied by a heartfelt caption, sharing the emotions behind the moments captured.

Daddy gazed at Mom then at me.

"What are you up to, girls? The doctor said I'm supposed to avoid strong emotions."

In reality, the doctor said nothing like that. He needed to run more tests and decide what was the best course to take. I cleared my throat.

"Well, Daddy, it's Christmas Eve, and we brought you a miniature Christmas tree," I said in the most cheerful voice I could fake and set a 15-inch tree complete with tiny decorations on the nearby table so he could see it. "Since you can't be at home tonight, this will add some holiday spirit. Some families open one gift on Christmas Eve. Your other gifts are at home, but since we're all here together, we thought you should open your first present."

A sparkle of joy lit Daddy's eyes and his voice regained the strength of a healthy man.

"Carolyn, would you please help me?"

Daddy pushed against his elbows, and Cheryl and I rushed to help him get into a sort of seated position as Mother arranged the two pillows behind his back. Then the three of us gathered around him. As he tore open the shiny gift paper and the gold ribbon fell on the floor, the magic of Christmas cloaked the room. The little book chronicled our life together.

It went like this:

Once there was a boy by a picture of Daddy as a young naval officer, *and a girl...* by a picture of Mom as a beautiful young woman, *Who fell in love...*

Then it highlighted me being born, and three years later, Cheryl. There were also photos of our family vacations, our dog, Prissy, ordinary moments, and funny moments. Somehow, all of us appreciated and realized the specialness of every moment we had shared. As we went through each page and commented on each picture, a new breath of life energized Daddy's body, and time stood still. Exclamations of joy and sweet memories enlivened the room, and I felt like a little girl again, joyous and carefree.

I saw him smiling from across the table during one of those fancy dinner parties Mother loved to throw, his head slightly turned so only I could notice the piece of spinach covering his upper front teeth. I remember having to look away and clench my jaws so I wouldn't roar with laughter.

Next, I was sneaking out of my bed to the living room late at night, and peeking out the window to see him come home from work, looking dashing in his Navy uniform. I loved the way he pushed open our white iron gate with a firm arm yet a gentle smile on his handsome face. However, it was my mother, the typical '50s housewife, who ran the show in our day-to-day life, an iron fist in a velvet glove. Mother was the one with a fancy car in our family, a rose-pink Lincoln that would have made Elvis jealous. In retrospect, my parents made a great team. Daddy was more supportive and fun, while Mother could be critical and demanding. However, he loved her just the way she was and bent over backward to please her. In the morning, Mother woke us up for breakfast, and Daddy made sure we had eggs and toast the way we loved it and drank our juice. Mother was always home when we came back after classes and close by the phone at 5:00 p.m. when Daddy called to let us know he was on his way home. Her face brightened with excitement as she got off the phone and ran back to freshen her lipstick. At 5:30 p.m. sharp, we heard the signature toot-toot of his horn as he rounded the corner to Robin Hood Lane.

Every evening, Cheryl and I had our Happy Hour together. Mom would make a snack, like chips and dip and a coke for Cheryl and I, and send us to the family room to watch television, while she and Dad had a cocktail or glass of wine to discuss their day. We all reunited for a cheerful dinner—a daily ritual — around the teal blue wrought iron glass-top table in the kitchen.

As I turned the last page of the photo album, Daddy's face beamed with joy, still handsome despite the sunken cheeks and meager body. I couldn't take my eyes off him, realizing how lucky we were to have him in our lives. He was such a beautiful being both outside and inside. His strong positive spirit, diplomacy, and knack for building rapport with everyone garnered respect and admiration. His constant ability to reinvent and better himself made a positive difference in people's lives, inspiring me to always be and do my best. He would be the soul of the party, excelling both on the dance floor and at the game table.

I started rubbing his feet, trying to give him the best foot massage ever. Cheryl held his hand and Mother kissed him gently on the lips. His eyes were sparkling with light, almost heavenly, his cheeks rosy. It truly was a moment of perfect love for our family. Daddy then said he had to go to the bathroom. My sister and I glanced at each other and stood up at the same time. He was a very modest person, and his hospital gown was open in the back. We did not want to embarrass him by being in the room when Mom helped him up.

As we stepped outside, from the corner of my eye, I saw him trying to get up.

"Carolyn, I'm falling down a tunnel," he cried.

Mother laid him back on the bed, and his eyes rolled upward as he passed out.

It was as if an ocean wave hit me hard and turned me upside down, leaving me disoriented and unable to recognize my surroundings. One doctor rushed in and then another and another until I stopped counting. I just stood in the hallway, my sweaty back against the ice-cold wall, my whole being silently screaming to God in a weird mix of anger and imploration. Inside the room, a male voice shouted, "Code Blue!" and others ran in to shock his heart.

My emotions and memories crumbled into one concise sentence. *"Please, save my father!"*

Alas, it was one of the few times when God didn't listen to my prayer. He had a different plan—a plan that broke my heart and put a big hole in my life.

Despite our hopes and prayers, the man who always lovingly got me without me having to say a word, was gone on December 24th, 1981 at 8:13 p.m.

The doctor looked at us and simply said,

"I'm sorry—we tried to save him, but we could not."

Daddy was only 54 years old. He was too young to die.

I drove Mother and Cheryl back to my parents' home in La Jolla. The three of us crawled into Mom's bed, still in shock and speechless. We hugged each other tightly, staring into the dark until we fell asleep.

That fateful night, Daddy appeared in Cheryl's dream, reassuring her he was fine. I remembered him sharing his dream a few weeks before, where Jesus had come to him to help him step into a new body, whole and strong. We had hoped it meant recovery, but it had turned out to be a premonition.

The same night, the prospect of spending the rest of my life climbing the corporate ladder higher and higher suddenly lost its luster. It was as if I was awakening my heart and soul from a deep slumber, reminding me of a promise I had made as a 12-year-old out of the blue.

We always had nice family dinners, and that night it was one of my favorites, steak and salad. I loved dipping my sourdough bread in the steak juice left on my plate. It was Cheryl's turn to do the dishes that night, and Mom had left the room for a phone call, so Daddy and I were by ourselves at the dinner table.

"Honey, what do you want to do when you grow up?" he asked me, a kind and loving look in his eyes.

I sat thoughtfully for a moment and listened deep inside for the answer. Suddenly, like a flash of light, I remembered something.

"I made a promise to use this life to help raise the consciousness of humanity," I said with authority.

Daddy looked at me blankly. I was baffled myself.

Where did that come from?

At 12, I wasn't even entirely sure what the word *consciousness* meant. However, I sensed it was something important that had to do with my destiny.

Was climbing the corporate ladder as a flight attendant supervisor with American Airlines and living in a posh condo in downtown San Diego the means by which I could elevate human consciousness? Or my destiny? Doubt crept in.

Inadvertently, Daddy had bestowed upon me one last gift, perhaps the most valuable of them all. His sudden and painful transition served as a wake-up call that eventually propelled me to aid millions of vulnerable children. Whenever I facilitate the finding of a new loving home for a child or the emancipation of a woman from the heavy chains of human trafficking, Daddy's presence comes to mind, assuring me he is smiling down from wherever he may be.

CHAPTER 1
NEW BEGINNINGS IN HAWAII

Happy days in Hawaii, 1990

IN THE AFTERMATH of Daddy's transition, I took a step backwards in my career by resigning from my high-paying management role at American Airlines and transitioning to a lower-paying job as a flight attendant. Some of my friends warned me I was making a big mistake, but to me it represented a forward step towards my Soul. The flexibility of my new job allowed me to delve into a heartfelt exploration of meaning and chart the course of my destiny.

First, I decided to go back to school although I already had a Master's Degree in Public Administration. The San Diego School of Integrative Studies, had a PhD curriculum in The Nature of Consciousness, and I enrolled in it. However, it took only a few classes for me to realize that academia was as big a trap as the corporate world. And so, I began to travel with the purpose of spiritual growth and documenting miraculous phenomena. For the next seven years, I traveled the world as a flight attendant and spiritual seeker. I didn't plan to do it for that long, but, with seven being the number of completeness and perfection, I needed all that time. Every Christmas on the anniversary of Daddy's death, Mother would join me, but usually I went alone.

I visited Grandfather David, spiritual elder of the Hopi, had psychic surgery in the Philippines, saw UFOs in the high Andes of Peru, and witnessed many miracles with Sai Baba in India, and in Medjugorje, Croatia. Regardless of their culture, religion, language, or spiritual practice, the teachers and masters shared the same message. We are Love. We are One. All these experiences changed me profoundly. I realized each of us is called to find a way, given our unique circumstances, to bring Love into action. I just needed to discover my way.

And that's when I received yet another phone call that would profoundly impact my life.

As my experience in the aviation sector grew, so did my awareness of the stark differences between myself and the other flight attendants. They didn't or couldn't understand why I was always reading spiritual books or sometimes fasted instead of feasting. But Cathy was somehow different. Although she loved wild parties and spent big money on fancy clothes, her heart was in the right place. Little gestures—like helping an older lady with her carry-on without being asked or giving a kid an extra bar of ice-cream to appease his anguish—showed a kind and considerate soul.

"American Airlines is opening a new flight attendant base in Honolulu. Imagine living in one of those posh high-rises in Waikiki! And gosh, the fancy nightclubs and restaurants!" she chirped at the other end of the line. "We'll have so much fun! What do ya' think?"

Her piece of news seemed a good omen. I wanted to get away from my comfortable life and be in a quiet place where I could hear God talking to me, telling me how I could bring love into action.

"It sounds great," I said. "I'm in.

"Then hurry up and submit your application. We're supposed to start in one month," she added and hung up.

I clutched the receiver tightly, my eyes fixed on the distant horizon where the azure sky merged seamlessly with the vast expanse of water. A wave of exhilaration swept through me. Teeming with tourists and abuzz with nightlife, Waikiki exceeded San Diego in its array of diversions. But who said I had to live in Waikiki?

In the wake of Cathy's call, I promptly listed my condo for sale. One of my girlfriends owned a tiny, tiny house on the North Shore of Oahu, about an hour and a half away from the airport, and she was looking for someone who could lease it from her for at least a year. That wasn't a coincidence. Instead of storing my belongings, I got rid of most of them. The accumulation of possessions ultimately becomes a weighty burden, and letting go of everything unnecessary, my body felt lighter, as if I had shed 20 pounds. I kept my flight-attendant uniform, a few bathing suits, my most special spiritual books and my car, which American Airlines shipped to the island.

Upon my arrival at Honolulu airport, the air, moist and thick against my face, was heavy with the scent of luscious plumeria and gardenia flowers, typical of tropical islands. A brilliant green parrot said *hello* with a cheerful squawk from atop a banyan tree, and the spotless cerulean sky announced another warm day. My mind went silent and my body relaxed as I realized it took so little to appreciate being alive.

As I drove through the pineapple fields and lush greenery all the way to the small village of Haleiwa, in Pupukea, a destination famous for the surfing championships, shave ice, and spectacular waves, my heart was singing. From the narrow winding road, I could see the cobalt blue ocean resting in the sunlight. Human silhouettes stood on top of a high rugged cliff at Waimea Beach Bay Park, and some of them would shoot their arms up to the sky straight like arrows, then plunge down into the waves. I couldn't wait to join them.

Despite being accustomed to my parents' expansive residence in La Jolla and my roomy condominium in San Diego, I wholeheartedly embraced my new living quarters immediately. Palm trees surrounded my new home, a white wooden cottage, with miles of beaches stretching in either direction and facing the magnificent Pacific. It was right in the impact zone of the infamous Banzai Pipeline, with some of the strongest surf in the world. It was only one room, with one tiny table and a bed, and not even a full kitchen, just a Bunsen Burner for a stove. The interior featured rough, unfinished wood that exuded a cozy and welcoming aura.

I enhanced the ambiance to resemble a Balinese shrine by incorporating pictures of Babaji, Jesus, Yogananda, and spiritual masters. A few holy books—"Serving Humanity, Quiet Mind, The Power of One, Autobiography of a Yogi", and a beautiful notebook since I loved journaling as a way of talking to God decorated my little nightstand. Necklaces, rosaries, and japamalas (I had lots of them—in different colors and stones) hung pretty much everywhere. When Mother first came to see me, she wanted to buy me a television, but there was hardly any room for it. The truth was, I didn't want a TV, as the music of the seagulls and pounding surf outside was the best entertainment show ever.

On the wild shores of North Hawaii, I practiced being totally in the Now—releasing old concepts of my body, my relationships, my past, my future. I surrendered to the incredible blessings in this chapter in the book of my life—the warm sun caressing my back and the waves embracing my thighs, the smell of the fresh salt air, the sound of my own bubbling laughter at the delight of the moment. Liberated from preconceived notions, every aspect of my being assumed cosmic importance. Every day, a new opportunity arose to release who I thought I was and allow my great shining Presence to fill my body and dictate each moment as it came. I could hear the guidance in my heart as an unerring answer to every question. Back in San Diego, I'd sleep until around 8:30 a.m., but here, the pounding of the waves woke me up earlier, even when I was off duty. Nature, my closest friend, was calling me.

When I didn't fly to Australia or New Zealand, I enjoyed living a simple life on the beach, away from the hustle and bustle of the modern world. Instead of hustling and doing things, I let myself just be—cradled and rocked by the waves, becoming dreamy, so I could receive the vision of my assignment from the inner planes.

I release you, mind, I would whisper. *Your life-depleting meanderings bore me.*

The ocean's blue crystalline and aquamarine waters filled me with joy, peacefulness, and sensuality. I bodysurfed in the powerful waves, swam with the turtles, and ran on the beach every day. The soothing sound of the waves crashing against the shore was a delightful lullaby as I drifted off to sleep.

But life at the beach in Hawaii had many other perks. The sight of the animals around the house brought a smile to my face. Geckos would sometimes show up on the kitchen floor or the porch, and in time, I learned to appreciate their company as silent and courteous roommates. Squeaker, a big black-and-white tomcat with mesmerizing green eyes, was another frequent guest in my home. We bonded over a piece of fried fish, and he returned every day, eager to be fed and petted.

I could go around my neighborhood on my baby-blue bicycle. My body could easily breathe, free from the constraints of fashion and makeup. I lived my life in a swimsuit, which I wore with a different color rayon or chiffon pareo (like a sarong) draped softly around my body, and often put flowers in my hair.

The bright pink swimsuit, with its high-cut sides, garnered me many compliments. It made me look like a model, people would say. On one moonlit night, I found myself on the brink of losing it—and also my life.

It was nearly 11 p.m., and I had just come home from a long trip to Auckland. However, the desire to meditate under the brilliant full moon kept me awake and prompted me to sit on my front porch as the mystical light sparkled off the pounding surf.

But Christian, a young, blond college guy taking care of Squeaker and the mansion siding my cottage, broke me from my reverie. He invited me for a midnight swim.

"Check out the ocean—a big set just came in…" he said.

I saw the glistening waves in the moonlight and accepted his invitation. What first looked like a gentle set of swells quickly became treacherous. As a California native, I knew how to ride waves, but this was nothing like the ocean back home. The waves threw me to the ocean floor and around and around until I did not know which way was up. A strong current tugged at my limbs, carrying me to the open waters, testing my muscles to the limit. I was thrashed around like a rag doll. It took me an hour to get back to the shore. It was only when I crashed onto the cool sand that I realized I was naked. Panting and shivering, I covered the front of my body with my arms. My eyes were moist with tears of joy at being alive and sadness at losing my favorite bathing suit. A couple of days later, Christian brought it back to me. A surfer had found it two miles down from where I lived.

Not too long after I moved to Hawaii, love knocked on my door again. Since my first love back in high-school, I established a Romeo-Juliet way of relating to men and had a series of intense relationships with boyfriends. In 1984, I journaled about the type of man I wanted as a partner.

He would be tall, have a nice athletic body, a pleasant smile, and beautiful eyes to exert that strong attraction on me I needed. His focus had to be first spiritual, and he would be involved in making the world a better place. Many people would look up to him. He would be adept at social graces and lots of fun to be around. He would also love to travel, cook, and eat delicious meals. He would be strong yet gentle, dedicated to his inner principles, trustworthy and willing to commit. He would be a wonderful, affectionate, and highly creative lover. And he would love children.

Jim was only some of it. He certainly had the looks—-6'2", slim, muscular, with his gentle soul shining from his big green–blue eyes—he turned heads at the beach or behind the counter at Jake's, a popular restaurant where he was bartending.

We met in line at Rosie's Coffee Shop. Rock'n'roll hits of the early '70s played softly in the background about love and loss, and people with tanned skin, cheerful smiles, and vivid-colored outfits conversed around small round tables. That's how all people in our neighborhood were, not just in Rosie's Coffee Shop—the hippie-type of people who enjoyed their life.

Jim was in line just in front of me. I noticed his height and scent, and the gentle aura that seemed to surround him like a cloud. A fan spun lazily from the dark brown wooden ceiling, making his salt-and-pepper ponytail flutter. It was an instant, unexpected attraction.

He ordered my favorite cinnamon-flavored coffee to-go in an absent voice, and I assumed something was on his mind. Perhaps a morning fight with his lover? Once he got his fix, he walked past me, as if I were invisible. But on my way out, I found him leaning against the door.

"Hi, I'm Jim," he said in a friendly, resonant voice, and took a long sip of coffee. "I see you like cinnamon as well. You must be new to Haleiwa. I haven't seen you around before. Let me know if you want me to come over to your place someday and cook you some cinnamon pie. I'm an excellent cook."

I smiled both at his audacity and the image of the face Mother would have made if she witnessed the scene. She had been harsh on Cheryl and me in our teenage years because she didn't want her girls to be *cheap*. Back then, I thought *cheap* meant *cool*, and she didn't want me to be cool. In fact, she didn't want either Cheryl or me to go the wrong direction, which could easily happen to a young girl in California in those days.

But this was Hawaii, and I was a young woman (although I wasn't looking for romance at the time.) There was something wild and sexy about Jim that swept me off my feet.

"Sure, are you free tomorrow? I live right on the impact zone of the Pipeline," I chirped, (knowing as a surfer he would know right where it was).

The next day, Jim arrived on time. Instead of a flower bouquet, he brought me a bag of groceries. I watched with awe as he expertly chopped garlic on the tiny cutting board, flamed the olive oil in the pan over the little Bunsen Burner, and chopped cilantro and onion into the veggies. He presented a delicious meal of Mahi-mahi with his special cous-cous flavored with rice wine vinegar. We ate dinner on the deck of my cottage, our eyes sparkling in the candlelight, and clicked our wine glasses in a toast to the setting sun in the glowing lavender light on the horizon.

"There's more!" he announced when our plates emptied. "I made you my special dessert. I call it "Jim's Surprise."

He disappeared into the kitchen and came out with a slice of luscious Mud Pie! This was my all-time favorite! How in the world did he ever know? It's made of graham cracker crust, a layer of chocolate, then coffee ice cream with whipped cream.

Jim slowly drizzled Kahlua and a little cinnamon over the top. I was mesmerized. He looked so tantalizing in his rayon faded blue Hawaiian shirt and strong, writhe, tanned body and his sexy wispy ponytail falling over his shoulder. When I closed my eyes in delight after the first bite, he bent over slowly and tenderly kissed the cream from my lips. I melted into the gentleness of his tender caress, and we became lovers.

Our life together unfolded like a perfect honeymoon. We loved hiking underneath the canopy of lush trees to hidden waterfalls, away from the beaten paths; riding our bikes through the pineapple fields; and going to coffee shops. We adored bathing naked in the ocean and loving each other with physical abandonment. We also shared the same taste for rayon: he wore rayon shirts, unbuttoned, and I swirly rayon Balinese dresses.

Jim and I also had a great time bantering and joking and having meaningful conversations where I would evoke my mission to bring love into action. Jim would listen carefully, then tell me stories about the Hawaiian gods and legends of sacred place on the islands, and we would spend hours musing over tiny shells in the sand.

Sometimes, I'd surprise myself thinking I could live like this—carefree, happy, adored—forever. We spent all our spare time together without ever getting bored.

Sometimes, I would go to Jake's restaurant while Jim was tending bar and have him make me a cocktail while I pretended I was just a customer. I would look at him behind the counter, at his ponytail and island clothes. I wondered what Mother would say if I married him. Ever since my first love, I always gravitated towards the men that others found unappealing and my parents disapproved of. It was my way of rebellion, a tangible manifestation of my longing to break free from the ordinary.

Jim was such a far cry from my educated, polished father, yet they had in common a selfless heart and deep love for me.

One night, a few months into our relationship, a terrible storm hit the North Shore, and the wild surf took big bites at the deserted beach. A strong wind pounded against the thin walls of my home as if trying to knock them down. A passionate surfer from a tender age, Jim had a small collection of pricey surfboards. He took great care of his "babies," polishing them and keeping them as new. And yet, he was willing to "sacrifice" one of them—as he put it—to save my little white house and appease the gods. I thought he was crazy, but he insisted on doing it. The ritual worked, and we didn't get wiped out. That's when I realized Jim loved me with all his heart and was serious about our relationship. But was I?

CHAPTER 2
THE MISSION IS REVEALED

Jim and I in my cottage on North shore of Oahu, Hawaii

I REVELED IN my simple life at the beach and my passionate romantic relationship, but every day, during my meditations, I pleaded with God to show me my mission, to reveal how I could make a difference. Arnie was one of his answers. With four days off each week, the idea of working part-time as a sales associate in a store that showcased vibrant clothes from Bali enticed me. The thought of immersing myself in a sea of colorful fabrics, hearing the soft rustle of garments, catching whiffs of exotic scents, and feeling the silky textures against my fingertips seemed like an absolute delight. In reality, it required immense dedication and labor to attend tirelessly to customers for a full eight-hour stretch and, as a result, I came to appreciate my flight attendant job more. One day, on my lunch break, I saw this old man sitting in the dirt, his back leaning against a palm tree. The vividness in his iridescent hazel eyes contradicted the wrinkles on his face, the dryness of his skin, and the silver in his long curly hair, as if a young boy hid inside his worn body. He wore a plain sleeveless T-shirt that must have been white once and a pair of khaki shorts. The soles of his flip-flops were paper thin. I had seen my share of homeless people in my life to recognize one and had made a pledge to comfort them in the best way I could. I walked up to him, and as soon as he introduced himself as Arnie, his stomach let out a low, rumbling growl.

"Excuse me, I haven't had a proper meal in days," he said, his eyes glued to his toes, black from dirt.

"But you are now! I'm taking you to lunch."

We walked to a little taco place around the corner and I invited him to order whatever he wanted. As we struck up a conversation, my guest spoke like an educated man, using the turn of phrases and words of an avid reader. He excelled at math and figuring things out. He could still run miles and climb a tree. But because he hated being caged, he had ended up living on the streets and beaches. With its beautiful weather, Hawaii was a great place to be homeless. Someone like him could pick fruit from the trees and jump into the ocean to clean his body.

Arnie baffled me at some point in our conversation.

"I just want to be. I don't want to make a difference."

(How could someone not want to make a difference?) The more I listened to him, the more I realized this man could have been anything, from a manual laborer to an office clerk. He deserved to have financial security and a roof over his head; I was determined to make it happen and help him find a job. I told him that, and he just shook his head, "Yep, yep," but he pursued none of the few opportunities I came up with. Two months later, his heart stopped beating. His passing weighed heavily on my heart, filling me with both sadness and guilt. I had blindly followed my vision of comforting him. Instead of accepting his choice, I had focused on *fixing* his situation. I thought I was loving while, in truth, I was trying to make him fit into my world and live according to my set of rules. Inadvertently, Arnie taught me to meet people where they were and allow them to be who they wanted to be. Maybe a deeper sense of love was just letting them be and setting them free. That applied to me as well.

When I sat still in meditation and really listened for what would truly elevate human consciousness, two things came to me. The first one was using mass media as a tool to give people a new perspective. Film and television could inspire (like modern day parables) and give millions of people a new and positive perspective. However, I wasn't in the film or TV business, so I wasn't sure how to leverage this medium. The second insight, right up my alley, was travel! Magic happened when people traveled because they stepped outside of their ordinary routine and were open to new experiences. Visiting unknown places changed how they looked at life. Many even fell in love!

My trip to the Hopi Reservation, after Daddy passed away, was a powerful example. There, upon awakening, we danced and chanted songs to the Great Spirit, sprinkling cornmeal on the ground instead of starting the day with reading the paper and listening to the news. Guided by Grandfather David, we connected with Mother Earth and Father Sky and our deepest and highest self. It was new, it was fresh, and it cracked my heart wide open. I became childlike again and remembered we were all connected to something bigger than ourselves.

Somehow, moving to Hawaii had done the same. It had broken me out of my ordinary routine. Away from the distractions of modern California, with its superficial glitter and endless parties, I could hear the voice of my soul. It was whispering to me that travel was and could be used as a tool to awaken consciousness. I wasn't in the travel industry by chance. I was put there to make a difference. No one was articulating a higher vision for the industry or had awareness of its potential for positive change and helping those in need.

What if my mission was to create a shift in consciousness by utilizing travel and involving flight attendants? By bringing love into action, they would feel the joy of aligning with their soul, far beyond the desire to possess things. As a community, we could become a catalyst for inspiring other travelers and make a global impact. As this idea crystalized, my heart sang with bliss, and a sense of calm and clarity washed over my mind—a sign of inspired action.

Synchronicities were another sign I was on the right track, and a major one was meeting Chris Belknap. This incredible man helped me take the first step on this beautiful journey I'm still on—-Airline Ambassadors International. Chris popped up in my life as soon as I started looking actively for a community of spiritual people I could connect with—the only thing missing from my heavenly experience in Hawaii. Our connection blossomed rapidly as we found a mental connection and shared a mutual understanding of human connectedness. Our mutual interest in spirituality also played a big part in our friendship. Not only could we have the most thought-provoking intellectual conversations but also chant Bhajans—holy Sanskrit hymns like Om Namah Shivaya—together. Chris enthusiastically supported my newfound vision for my mission, offering to use his graphic design skills to create a visually captivating written proposal for American Airlines. My previous efforts to make my voice heard had been unsuccessful. Just before leaving for Hawaii, I had attended a Town Hall meeting of Mr. Crandall, President and CEO of American Airlines, and afterwards wrote him a letter. He was known as a ruthless and competitive leader, but also capable and strong. In my letter, I suggested American Airlines adopt a triple-win philosophy that would help stockholders, travelers, and the world alike and propel AA as a number one airline by adopting a larger vision for the industry.

I'll never forget his reply.

"We seek one thing at American, and one thing alone - and that is to vanquish all other airlines."

Oh my God, what a Neanderthal!

It was discouraging to work for someone who couldn't see how a wider vision could push the company forward. However, with Chris's input and design skills, I hoped Mr. Crandall would be more inclined to consider my ideas. There was not really physical chemistry between Chris and me (he was a nice looking all-American with a heavy-set frame), yet the more time we spent together, the further away I drifted from my boyfriend, Jim. A mission was gradually unveiling itself to me, a way to make a meaningful impact, which demanded my utmost dedication to pursue it. Yet, it was hard to break up. Something major had to happen to make me walk away. And by major, I don't mean bad.

It must have been over a year since I had moved to Hawaii. It was on those rare evenings when Jim and I were at the beach, bathed in the moonlight. We were sitting in silence and awe, our bodies in a tight embrace. When you cultivate an appreciation for the precious now moment, you naturally gravitate away from any potential distractions. You don't want to miss the threads of golden awareness and richness of love that life masterfully weaves together.

Jim slowly unwrapped his arms from my waist, cupped my face with his big rough hands, and looked me straight in the eye.

"I need to tell you this right now," he stammered.

"To ask you. Nancy, I love you! I know you have a mission, and I will support you. How should I put it? Nancy, I don't have a ring…. Yet… but I want you to be my wife!"

I was shocked. Although the moment was magical and part of me wanted to go along with the fantasy, I reached deep inside and knew I did not want to make a mistake in who to marry. I knew I was on this planet for more than my own happiness. I had made a promise before coming into this life, and I had to stay true to it. If I were to enter wedlock, it would be solely on the grounds of our shared mission.

"No!" I pounded my fist against the sand. "I have a mission, and nobody's going to stop me."

"Nancy, I can take care of you! I know you have a special purpose and I will support you, cook for you and be there for you. Don't worry," he insisted. But the magic of the evening was gone. I brought myself to a standing position and marched to my cottage. Part of me was relieved. Part of me was sad,

How could he not get it? I didn't require someone to care for me, but rather a man capable of joining me in making a positive impact in the world. I had to stay true to my inner voice even if I had to give up my greatest temptation—the love and fulfillment I found in a romantic relationship.

With each of my boyfriends, I had succumbed to the enchanting allure of the Siren of Love and found myself ensnared in a deceitful sense of security for extended periods. I always thought I needed the love of a man because I doubted I was good enough alone.

I still had a considerable distance to cover before little Nancy, concealed within a woman's physical form, could ultimately restore the self-assurance that was fractured during her early years. My younger sister, Cheryl, was born when I had the measles. The newborn, so fragile and unequipped for this world, took up all my parents' attention. But I couldn't know that, nor did they explain it to me. I felt frantic at being ignored, unloved, and not good enough. That was probably my first lesson in neglecting my own feelings and making everyone happy instead.

When Chris asked for my help in organizing his upcoming Youth Summit in Honolulu, I found the perfect excuse to leave Haleiwa and to put some distance between Jim and me.

As the state capital and largest city in Hawaii, it was the perfect place for making new connections with officials, NGOs, and business people in positions of influence. Some of them, my heart told me, would surely use their power for the good of others.

But giving up my idyllic, tropical life meant more than pursuing my mission. I was overcoming one of my biggest weaknesses and learning how to stand on my own two feet without a romantic partner. Escaping was my means of cementing my determination.

I located a small cottage on Kinau St. within walking distance from Ala Moana Park and close to Chris Belknap's place and moved my holy books, rosaries, japamalas, bathing suits, and flight attendant uniforms to a new life.

The first few weeks were tough. I missed hearing the pounding of the waves just outside my window. The softness of the pillow

I hugged to go to sleep paled compared to Jim's brawny arms wrapped around my body in a tender embrace. Yet, during the day, my flight attendant job and the upcoming Youth Summit kept my mind busy. In fact, I was so excited about the event that I shared it with one of my friends from Moscow. His name was Joseph Golden, and I had met him during my spiritual search years ago when I was traveling in the former Soviet Union. Joseph worked with Buckminster Fuller and helped coordinate the first "Space Bridge" between Moscow and San Francisco in 1989. Staged by the Soviet government and a US peace group called World Beyond War, the videoconference connected 4,000 Americans and 3,000 Russians to use the power of satellite telecommunications to foster world peace. Joseph loved Chris's idea for a Youth Summit and inspired me to solicit AT&T to donate four video phones. Amazingly, AT&T agreed to do it. It may seem hard to believe now, but video phones were an amazing and rare technology in 1989. I kept one for Honolulu and used my airline discount to send the others to our contacts in Moscow, London, and Sydney. Chris included a videoconference as part of the program.

For an entire day, 300 students in Honolulu envisioned what a better world would look like: environmentally, economically, and culturally. In the afternoon, they were invited to sit in the dignified, plush chairs in the Hawaii State Senate. I prayed the videophones would work, as students in Moscow, London, and Sydney were waiting to connect with us.

We started the call with Moscow. Everyone was staring at the huge black screen in front of the room. There was some static and then, suddenly, the picture of a young boy came on. He was in black and white and spoke in broken English with a heavy Russian accent, but everybody was smiling with excitement.

"Hello, my name is Mischa, and we have 200 students here in Moscow who have been thinking about what a world that works for everyone would look like…"

"Hi, Mischa!" cried the voices of 300 kids in the Hawaii State Senate auditorium, rising up as one chorus, bringing tears to my eyes. There was much love filling up that room and traveling the distance to Moscow and then returning to us, tenfold. How strange! I had never experienced such a strong feeling of utter joy, enthusiasm, and fulfillment outside a romantic relationship, but here I was, living it with people I barely knew. I didn't need a man to experience love. To be fulfilled. I realized that fulfillment happened when we followed the calling of our Souls.

The rest of the day only confirmed it. We connected with the kids in Sydney and those in London. As they exchanged ideas, these young people on three different continents realized they were not so different. They all had the same basic goals and dreams, and united, they could change the world. United, we can change the world. This was such a profound moment for me; I saw telecommunications were the face-to-face corollary of travel. As we jubilantly celebrated the success of the Youth Summit over a delectable late dinner, a persistent question incessantly lingered in my mind, accompanied by the clinking of glasses, the aromatic wafts of savory delicacies, and an overwhelming sense of accomplishment.

What if I could impact people from all over the world, regardless of their nationality and skin color? And what better opportunity to find out if not at the upcoming United Nations Earth Summit.

CHAPTER 3
THE POWER OF SAYING NO

Listening for guidance

I'VE ALWAYS HAD mentors. They gave me strength and courage, inspired me to take the next step, and enabled me to see beyond my blind spots. My Dad was the first one, although inadvertently, with his love for life, grace, poise, and people skills. He was among the very few who stayed with me until now and will continue to stay, even from beyond the threshold to the other world.

As I evolved, the Universe brought to me those who were right for me at that time in my life and stage of growth. A name dropped at a gathering or friendly meeting would stay with me, and I knew I had to read the book, listen to the interview, or, in most cases, meet that person. Even as a teenager, a keen interest and curiosity about people doubled my dreamy nature—so inclined as I was to look beyond the veil of our daily life.

During my summer jobs at the La Jolla Tennis Club, I ended up knowing almost everybody. The guests seemed to gravitate to tall, slender, blue-eyed girls like me, and I loved listening and learning from their stories. In the early '90s, Dr. Robert Mueller, retired UN Under Secretary General; Rashmi Mayur, President of the Global Future Society; Elisabet Sahtouris, environmental scientist; and Hazel Henderson, famous economist, were fueling and shaping my vision of what our world could be. They were also talking about the Windstar Aspen Conference and the Earth Summit as life-changing events, and I couldn't wait to attend both and hoped American Airlines would see the potential of getting involved as well.

Inspired by the upcoming conferences, I called American Airlines Marketing to schedule a meeting. The events, combined with the days and nights Chris Belknap and I had put into my new proposal, were paying off. Henry Joyner, head of Marketing at American Airlines, agreed to meet me at AA's headquarters near DFW Airport.

A rainbow was arching over the high rises in downtown Honolulu as I boarded the plane to Dallas Fort Worth, my lucky green suit neatly folded inside my carry-on. I took it as a good omen, and prepared for the eight-hour journey. After a refreshing night's sleep at the airport Hilton, I arrived at American Airlines Headquarters that morning. My heart pounded like crazy as I stepped inside Henry Joyner's office. The city stretched for miles and miles outside the glass walls behind his desk in a symphony of glass, steel, and concrete. Observing a landscape from high up in the sky was nothing new to me, yet this time it felt different. The sight of this urban area pulsating with life, filled with the hopes and dreams of millions of people, waved at me like an invitation to play big and finally step into my role.

Joyner shook my hand briefly and invited me to sit down in the huge black leather swivel chair across from his desk. I thanked him for his time and pulled out the presentation from my briefcase. I was so proud of it—not just of the ideas, but also of the professional design with elegant graphics and professional pictures that would have made even an ad man jealous. The man leafed through it for a few seconds and, with an amused smile on his face, invited me to speak.

"Since you came all the way here from Honolulu, why don't you explain to me what's all this about?"

"Of course," I said in an excited voice. If somebody would have awakened me in the middle of the night and asked me to talk about my vision, I would have happily done it. "You'll love this, I promise!"

I handed Henry the elegant light gray overview booklet with a round sticker of the Earth from space in the center (that Chris and I had worked so hard on) and explained how American Airlines would bring in new customers and build trust and loyalty with the existing ones by making a positive impact in the world. Additionally, my program would incentivize flight attendants to help children around the world by hand-delivering aid and volunteering at international conferences. It would create built-in media that would win the hearts and minds of customers, stakeholders, politicians, and players in the business community. I had in mind passengers who wanted to travel and do good and organizers of environmental and UN conferences.

Joyner shook his head, listened politely, and not once interrupted me, not even with a question. By the time I suggested American Airlines become a sponsor of the Earth Summit, he had almost tricked me into believing he was interested, so I continued:

"Through my personal connections, I can bring in 4,000 people that would book American Airlines to fly to this important and historic United National Conference. Most of the world's presidents are attending. CEOs of the top global companies, non-governmental organizations, and indigenous leaders are taking part, as well as spiritual leaders."

I had been talking for 40 minutes straight, and my mouth felt dry and my throat a little sore, but I expected an enthusiastic yes. Joyner had to see the opportunity. Even someone less business-savvy would have. But silence enveloped the room.

He's overwhelmed, Nancy, he's just impressed and maybe trying to figure out whom to call first to set things in motion.

"This sounds great, but it doesn't really fit with our vision, our policy" he said slowly, as if he wanted to let every word sink in and make sure I would never bother him again.

"If you want us to give you a few tickets to help children, we may do that," he threw me a bone. To him, I was just a flight attendant—a funky chick who dared him with a new business model totally different from his CEO's vision of "vanquishing" every other airline. He wasn't in the least bit interested in his own flight attendants making a difference. Prisoners of the old patterns, Joyner and executives at American Airlines were turning a blind eye to the cultural trends of the day where people gave their loyalty and money to companies that cared.

When he looked at his watch, stood up and thanked me in an empty voice, I was devastated.

Would the world ever see me for who I really was and the power of the ideas I was sharing?

As the cab took me to the airport, my past flashed in front of my eyes. Seventh grade again, missing a bunch of questions on purpose because kids who seemed cool didn't pass the test and I wanted so badly to be cool.

Grandfather David sneaking his hand under my skirt during my trip to Hopiland only a few years ago. Maybe it was my fault, and my dream of measuring up to the people I so much admired—-people who had the means, the notoriety, and power to make a positive change in the world—-was unrealistic. I wished I still had my tiny white cottage on the North Shore of Hawaii and Jim's arms around me, his words of endearment softly spoken in my ear.

Silently, I asked the Creator to send me a sign.

He did. He sent me Sarah. We were ready for takeoff, all passengers in their seats, when a little Asian girl in the aisle seat across from mine started sobbing because she had lost her favorite doll. Her mother gave her a quick hug and whispered something in her ear. The wailing stopped, but tears still rolled down her smooth cheeks. Like a good fairy, a flight attendant scurried by with chocolate ice cream in her hand. Sarah was the name on her tag. She must have been in her late forties, but still looked gorgeous. She crouched by the little girl, her eyes glowing, and handed her the tasty dessert. As the child confessed it was her first time on an airplane, Sarah reassured her by making up a story about invisible superheroes safely carrying the plane on their wings to our destination in Honolulu. I couldn't take my eyes off of them. I told myself there must have been other flight attendants like Sarah and scared little children who needed their help. And I simply dreamt, while being fully awake. By the time our superheroes landed the plane, resolve had replaced the sadness and dejection caused by Joyner's pushback.

After a few days in Honolulu, I packed my warmest clothes (in Aspen it gets cold after sundown in September) and, accompanied by my good friend Chris Belknap, flew to Aspen, Colorado. The conference was open to everyone and we were excited to be part of it.

What better place for a gathering of the brightest minds and the most beautiful souls on the planet (or so I thought at that time) than the breathtaking Rocky Mountains and their crown jewel in Colorado, Aspen? The four-day Windstar conference, founded by musician John Denver, drew nearly 1,000 environmentalists to hear lectures and plot strategies to save the planet. Bonus: live music and real espresso. Chris and I were thrilled to hang out with Barbara Marx Hubbard, Marianne Williamson, Bill Galt, luminaries, and visionaries we admired, as well as celebrities, including Olivia Newton-John, Whoopi Goldberg, and John Denver himself. His opening statement at the conference pointed out our responsibility, as a highly evolved species, to preserve Earth and life.

"Within the next decade, and certainly within our lifetimes, we're going to determine whether the Earth remains habitable for higher life forms," he said.

The presentations and speeches buzzed with enthusiasm and passion, emphasizing one of my guiding credos — we are interconnected not just with nature but also with us as people. Some of the participants astonished me with their willpower and dedication to a noble cause. One of my fondest memories was meeting Paul Coleman. This extraordinary man had walked from Canada to Aspen and was planning on continuing his walk all the way to the Earth Summit in Rio de Janeiro to draw attention to the destruction of the world's forests.

While the majority of the delegates were lodged in hotels, Chris and I stayed in a big house that belonged to one of his friends. Its enormous living room with high glass sliding doors leading to a round outdoor patio was a perfect place for gatherings.

The Windstar Aspen Summit turned out to be an eye opener in many ways. It showed me that the powerful, rich, spiritual, at the top of the social ladder had no intention of using their wealth and influence to make a positive change in the world at a big level. Sure, their words sounded nice and promising, but their actions spoke a different language.

Case in point: one late evening, my mentor and friend, Bill Galt, had organized a special gathering. Many of the rich and famous people I deeply admired were there. Soon after about 20 people arrived, I noticed the heavy scent of incense filling the sizable room. The floor was covered in thick rugs and soft music ran in the background. Plates with exotic fruits and figs and jugs of lemon water and tea garnered a buffet hidden behind a violet gazebo. Bill confided that we were not just there to talk about ideas for a better world—-this was an Ayahuasca ceremony! Before taking the magic potion, we had a little tea. I was kind of nervous since I had never tried it before. I knew Shamans warned Ayahuasca wasn't something to play with. On the contrary, it was something to be respected and taken under the surveillance of a seasoned healer. It was a guide to one's inner deepest depths, beyond their shadow and limitations, into the real self. It had the power to alter life for good and restore the authentic self. I knew it would normally help the body purge toxins and old residues and wondered what would happen when everybody in the room would start puking their guts out.

However, none of that happened, maybe because the intention behind the ceremony was different. As my body started tingling and a strange sensation of warmth embraced every limb, a Tantra teacher entered the room. She wore a long white tunic on her bare skin and a violet crystal gleamed between her eyebrows. The volume on the loudspeaker turned louder, and she started to dance. Slowly, her graceful movements became an act of self-love, and she started touching herself. The men in the room reached out for the women next to them, eager to please and be pleased. I sat on a soft pillow on the floor in the lotus position, inert as a statue.

Unfortunately, I realized that many of those I admired were motivated by personal gain and driven by sensual purposes, by the desire for worldly experience, even a psychedelic one. Instead of stretching their capacity to build a new humanity, they were indulging in their wildest passions. They were using this event to explore their sensuality, not build a new civilization.

Only my eyes felt alive, scrutinizing the room as if another me was watching the entire scene as a silent observer. Eventually, unknown icy fingers touched my thigh and life came back to my body. I jumped on my feet and left the room, clutching a small picture frame with a portrait of Babaji (whom I had hoped could guide me).

I started the next day at sunrise in meditation, while the participants in the ceremony were still lying asleep in the room. Sadly, I saw the truth that those I had admired were using drugs to indulge their fantasies. Who was going to save the world? We could not rely on others to do it.

If those rich, famous, powerful people didn't care, on whom was that task going to land? I had the startling realization that it was people like me, ordinary people, driven by the true calling of their souls! Although I was not rich or powerful, I knew I had to, at least, try to make a difference; my motivation was at least sincere. As daunting as it was, this realization rang true.

Luckily, I was not alone in my endeavor. When we pursue our destiny, we always get help. There were a few good people among the powerful and famous, and one of them was Rennie Davis. Best known as an American anti-war activist of the '60s, he was one of the Chicago Seven defendants charged for anti-war demonstrations and large-scale protests at the 1968 Democratic National Convention in Chicago. Each time he walked into a room, everybody cheered for this self-assured man of medium build. By that time, his hair was cut shorter than in the pictures I'd seen in the newspaper and his forehead looked really tall behind his short fringes. For the remaining days of the conference, our paths crossed often. Each time I felt a slight fluttering in my soul. Chris and I decided to have a gathering before leaving Aspen to map out a game plan of how we could all work together.

On my guest list, I included Rennie Davis and Sasha White. Both accepted our invitation. I had met Sasha in Costa Rica at the Seeking the True Meaning of Peace conference. An inspiring visionary, she was guided by her heart and founded the Campaign for the Earth, an NGO. Overall, we had about 40 guests who gathered in our big living room, which looked out onto the patio and cool fire pit.

We took turns introducing ourselves. Everyone had an amazing story, but when Rennie began speaking, I was riveted. His voice was rich with a certain spiritual authority.

"This is a time of the Great Turning. It's our time to capture the imagination of the human race and to launch the largest global movement in history. I am asking all of you to join me in building a Campaign for the Earth," he said.

His words triggered a big AHA moment for me.

This is it. By partnering with like-minded and dedicated others I can bring love into action and protect Mother Earth and her children. Maybe involve some flight attendants to help. Mother Earth is home to us all, regardless of gender, race, age, or social status, and I've always had this deep connection with her. She supports us unconditionally and blesses us with her gifts. We need to take care of her—preserve and honor her—just as she takes care of us.

Sasha and I agreed to work with Rennie to plan the Campaign for the Earth debut at the Earth Summit happening in Rio de Janeiro in June 1992. For 14 consecutive days, the event hosted a number of meetings including The United Nations Conference on Environment and Development (UNCED) for Presidents and other officials; the Global Forum for NGOs; the Wisdom Keepers; and a forum for indigenous peoples too. Chris agreed to launch a simultaneous campaign in Hawaii. We left Aspen on a high and decided to call our movement Rolling Thunder.

I've long forgiven Henry Joyner of American Airlines for his heart-breaking no. In doing so, he forced me to be more creative and open up to all the avenues the Universe had prepared for me to assist me on my mission. It forced me to think big, beyond one airline, to how I could make a difference.

CHAPTER 4
DAVE

Dave...

SASHA AND I had met Dr. Rashmi Mayur at the Seeking the True Meaning of Peace meeting in Costa Rica. He was a brilliant intellect and a mentor to both of us - we told him of our plan. He loved the idea of Rolling Thunder and recommended we register

Campaign for the Earth as an NGO with the United Nations and attend the preparatory meeting before the Earth Summit happening in New York. He also assisted us in applying and agreed to be a speaker at our event in Rio.

My gut was telling me that every piece of his advice was right and I needed to follow his instructions. Without thinking twice, I dropped my upcoming trips as a flight attendant to accommodate two trips to the Big Apple.

I could only afford a room at the Vanderbilt YMCA, a cheap hotel but two blocks away from the United Nations. The place was stark, and I hated sharing a bathroom, but I was away most of the day, so it didn't really matter. The first step was to get my credentials as a UN Representative. I attended all the meetings, conversations, and panels where my badge would get me access. Unlike the rich and famous in Aspen, the people here were sincerely planning on how they could better the world and taking the preparations for the Summit very seriously. For the first time in months, my inner turmoil was calming down knowing that I had finally found my tribe. Agenda 21 and the significant work that needed to be done to create a global plan to move the world to sustainability by 2021 was one of the things that struck me the most, giving me food for thought and inspiration, especially since so many sophisticated NGOs were already taking action and were way ahead of us.

"Rennie and Sasha, a lot of people are out there already working on these issues. Let's find a way to collaborate rather than launching a whole new movement." I shared with Rennie and Sasha once I returned to Boulder. They listened politely, but seemed intent on sticking to their original plan.

Rennie planned to arrange a large tent for Campaign for the Earth at the Global Forum, which gathered 317 NGOs and drew thousands of visitors. In fact, Rennie had an even more off-the-wall idea. He wanted me to be the Master of Ceremonies (MC) for the full two weeks at the Campaign for the Earth tent at the Global Forum. Every day we would publish a list of speakers. In total we had over a hundred speakers giving presentations every hour, from early morning until late afternoon.

"Oh, no, Rennie! It should definitely be you or Sasha," I replied.

"No, you are the one. I want you to do it," said Rennie. One doesn't argue with him!

Secretly, I was thrilled, although it would stretch all my abilities to act as hostess, welcoming so many guests with a powerful breadth ranging from Jerry Brown, Elisabet Sahtouris, Hazel Henderson, David Suzuki and Aritina Yataguarini, Chief of the Yanomami, for the two-week Earth Summit.

June 3, 1992, the first day of the Earth Summit arrived quickly. I had convinced my flight attendant friend Teri Sherrow, from Hawaii, to travel with me. The many seats open on the American Airlines plane were a sad reminder of Joyner's short-sightedness. American Airlines could have booked those seats, received the revenue, and made a huge difference in the world.

I broke out of my daydreaming as soon as we deplaned. The airport was packed with indigenous peoples, environmentalists, and activists. The heads of state had a separate exit, of course. In fact, The Earth Summit brought together 118 heads of state, making it the most significant UN gathering since its inception in 1945.

I was bursting with excitement at being part of such a historic gathering, and so was everybody around me. I had no clue (yet) that this event would change my life dramatically. However, I should have known based on the synchronicities that started manifesting early on while we were still up in the air. Synchronicities typically happen when we are fulfilling our destiny and are on our right path.

During the flight, I struck up a conversation with a man called Adnan Sarhan. I didn't know he was a renowned Sufi teacher and the official opening act for the Earth Summit. But he was nice, grounded, and saw my true self.

"You have a lot of inner light and you could increase that if you took one of my classes. Why don't you come join me at the Wisdom Keepers Retreat on Thursday at 4 p.m.?" he asked while we were waiting for our luggage in Baggage Claim. I eagerly agreed, excited to meet him again, and he nodded in contentment. Our conversation would have continued for hours if a confident, attractive woman with lots of charisma hadn't walked up to us.

"Adnan, I am so glad you made it safely," she said warmly. "Come with me. I have arranged your transportation."

"That must be Hanne Strong," I whispered to Teri.

I had heard about the gathering she had arranged for spiritual leaders. Hanne was the wife of the Secretary General, Maurice Strong. We watched Adnan join a group of dignitaries from all over the world. Swami Ji, Yogi Ranjeet, Chief Oren Lyons, Vandana Shiva and African activist Wangari Maathai were among them.

"Oh, I just wish WE could have been invited to the Wisdom Keepers gathering," I said to Teri

"Maybe we will. You have this knack, Nancy, for thinking about something and making it become reality almost instantly. Let's go. Rio is expecting us," Teri winked at me.

Outside the airport, the air was warm and moist, and loud voices fused with raspy honks and the rumbling of rolling luggage. We eventually escaped it to the inside a beaten-up cab. I had tried to get a hotel room at Hotel Gloria, the place where many of the people who were notable were staying, but it had no availability. However, we asked the driver to take us there, just to check the action, before we went to our hotel, further downtown. We paid the driver and stepped into the lobby pulling at our bulky bags—we needed clothing for two weeks.

We were wide eyed just looking at the lobby - Presidents, NGO representatives, spiritual leaders, corporate leaders, indigenous people, everybody was in Rio, and many of them were staying at Gloria Hotel. Ted Turner, Jane Fonda, Olivia Newton John, and Al Gore, to name a few.

Terri's carry-on flipped to the tile floor with a bang. A tall good–looking guy with white hair passing by stopped to help us. He introduced himself as Benton Musselwhite, an oilman from Houston, founder of One World Now, and the one funding the Indigenous People's Summit. He was talking to both of us, but his eyes were set on my white cotton sweater with open weave to the fuchsia silk camisole beneath.

"Well, I have some extra rooms reserved at the Gloria Hotel, and you two little darlins absolutely need to be here!," as he concluded his introduction in a slow Southern drawl. "And you are cordially invited to attend the opening of the Indigenous People's Summit, which opens tonight at 7 p.m. in the Plenary Hall upstairs!"

Teri threw me one of her *I told you so glances,* and answered for both of us:

"That's very kind of you! We'll stay."

"See you at 7 p.m.!" I added quickly, pulling myself together from receiving this unexpected boon. My special connection with the native people had become even stronger after my time with the Hopi Indians. I admired them for their spirit, traditions, and profound connection with Mother Nature and the Earth.

"Did you see the way the guy was eyeing you?" Teri exclaimed when there were just the two of us in the elevator." I nodded with a smile. I was so used to it, it didn't bother me anymore. "I bet you'll find a husband by the time we leave," she joked.

I laughed softly.

A husband. The thought was appealing but no longer at the top of my priority list.

"We shall see…"

We skipped dinner despite the loud churning in our stomachs and, at 7:00 p.m. sharp, entered the big auditorium reserved for the opening ceremony of the Indigenous People's Summit. Just as Benton had promised, our names were on the guest list. Representatives of native tribes across the world packed the place. Oren Lyons, the legendary leader of the Onondaga Nation in the US, was there as well as leaders of tribes throughout Brazil. The meeting lasted long, with many speeches that captivated most of the audience. The intentions and messages were all good and positive, but the setting and language a bit too formal for the indigenous people, who were used to vast open spaces. They were used to living sustainably, in harmony with nature, and not comfortable in a big auditorium. We have a lot to learn from them. There were about 200 gathered in a special section of the auditorium, a splash of color because they all were wearing beautiful traditional headdresses and some even had the plates in their lips.

At some point, I noticed open seats where they were supposed to be. This was their meeting, but they had left! I wondered what happened and hoped I'd get a second chance at being introduced to them. As I found out later, they got bored, went into the reception area, ate most of the shrimp, gathered up the souvenir T-shirts and took a walk on the beach. The media actually caught on camera dozens of Yanomami in their colorful headdresses, wearing One World Now T-shirts, wandering down the beach at about 10 p.m.!

During the dinner party the following night, I bumped into Elizabeth Spens, whom I had befriended at the Preparatory Conference in New York, accompanied by a good looking man in his mid-forties. He glanced at me in admiration. I was going to wear something simple, but had a last-minute change of heart and put on a new elegant purple dress.

"Nancy, I want to introduce you to Dave," Elizabeth said in a solemn voice, as if she were introducing me to the president of the United States.

"Nice meeting you, Nancy," he said, and I loved the sound of his voice and the presence in his eyes. *Oh, here's a nice guy,* I told myself.

"Are you staying at Hotel Gloria?" I asked.

"I have a room at the Gloria, but I am letting my indigenous friend Ariatne Wylapete stay there instead of me. Hanne Strong invited me to stay at the Wisdom Keepers Retreat."

I couldn't believe it. First of all, I guessed right. The woman at the airport was Hanne Strong. Of all the places, Wisdom Keepers was where I wanted to be the most, yet Dave was the one to go. He'd get to meet and talk to the brightest spiritual leaders on the planet. Was he as passionate about spirituality as I was? I decided I'd find out.

"Oh, you are so lucky," I replied. "How in the world did you get invited?"

"Well, I'm not sure. I met Hannah when I was working on the National Environmental Protection Act with Bella Abzug in 1972 and we have been friends ever since. The California Foundation and Environmental Grantmakers I am representing helped fund many environmental initiatives in the Bay Area. Maybe they see me as representing resources?"

He laughed at himself good-naturedly, and suddenly I liked him.

I gave him the business card I had made for the conference: Nancy Larson, Campaign for the Earth.

"Do drop by our tent at the Global Forum. It's one of the largest there," I said invitingly.

"Well, I'll mainly be at the UNCED headquarters with the Heads of State, but if I can get to the Global Forum, I will check it out."

This guy was fascinating and especially so, because he was nice, but I didn't catch his interest in me as a woman. He wasn't like Benton Musselwhite.

A few days later, Dave and I ran into each other again by accident.

Teri and I followed up on the invitation from Adnan Sarhan to take his Sufi class and jumped in a cab to visit the lovely Wisdom Keepers retreat, where all the spiritual luminaries were staying, about 20 minutes from Hotel Gloria.

Orchids and other exotic flowers, perfuming the air in a beautiful, natural setting. I thought we were going to learn Sufi dancing and be moving about, but Adnan had our group of 20 participants in his class simply breathe—a deep conscious breathing — after conversing for a few minutes. The deep breaths went on for at least 30 minutes. It's amazing how this practice can shift awareness.

"Now you're in the state where you can direct time," he told us.

I was so peaceful, in a high state of consciousness and deep oneness. I also sensed the people in a state of ordinary "monkey mind" and how scattered they were. Relaxed and at peace, I sat on a bamboo bench outside the retreat in front of bright pink geraniums just being in the NOW and gazing at the beautiful gardens.

Dave Rivard walked up unexpectedly from my left and said, "Hello."

I noticed sparkles around his head and immediately knew he was a special person. *I wanna hang out more with this guy*, I decided, realizing he was in the same state of consciousness as myself.

When I saw him later on in the company of a girl who was working for him, I felt a little jealous. She was dressed to the nines, smiling and bubbly, obviously trying to seduce him. But with the Campaign for the Earth's events just around the corner, I couldn't dwell on it.

I didn't prepare for my appearances as an MC, although I got to introduce big names like Al Gore, Wangari Matthai, and Elizabeth Sahtouris. I just allowed my intuition and inspiration to guide me. Whenever I'd get nervous, I'd tell myself they were people, just like me. I loved working with Teri, too. She was always at the back of the tent and acted like my right-hand person. She was strong, and I was diplomatic; we made a great team.

Overall, it felt like I was in the right place, and I was good at what I was doing. Not for a second was I tired and bored. How could I have been? As the MC for the event and listening to some of the brightest minds on the planet and observing how they were all connected? To this day, I'm deeply grateful for this opportunity. The politicians, businessmen, scientists and charities, each had their own ideas, but they were all tuning in to the same inner inspiration for building a new civilization based on the reality of our connectedness to one another and the Earth. As the Kogi Indians say, *"It is the destiny of humankind to become a gardener for the world. Not only for the physical world, but for "Aluna", the spiritual atmosphere that connects us all."* Our daily schedule included eight speakers and ended with great parties at night with singing, dancing, and drumming.

Those were two of the most magical weeks of my life. It seemed that with so many gathered together similarly motivated, synchronicities increased for all of us. We would think about something and it would happen, not only once, but again and again.

I had a close brush with death during the Earth Summit. Before I even landed in Rio, I'd heard rumors about police shooting the street kids to clean up the streets of Rio before the Summit. I refused to believe it. I couldn't wrap my head about the idea of adults killing innocent children in cold blood. Later, as AAI began its relentless fight against human trafficking, I learned that grown-ups harmed kids in more horrendous ways, which scarred them for life if they survived.

I knew how poverty-stricken the people of Rio were and how children often went to bed with an empty stomach. Therefore, during my first longer break from my schedule, I grabbed Teri and headed to the favelas. We packed our large backpacks with donations we had collected from our layovers: hygiene items such as soaps, shampoos and lotions, as well as cinnamon cookies from the airplane.

The air was thick with the scent of rotting garbage, but the kids were grateful for any small gifts and surrounded us. Their round, black eyes lit up in surprise when they saw us. We looked nothing like the cruel police officer chasing them downtown to end their lives.

I was especially touched by meeting Esmerelda. She looked to be about 10 years old. There was just something in her eyes. We told her and her friends about the Concert on June 14th, the Grand Finale of the Earth Summit, on the beach, and invited them to join us.

We almost started a riot because gangs ran through those hoods. They hated being photographed. Teri snapped a picture of the kids, capturing also the menacing bulky man in the distance. He looked young, in his 20s maybe, and sported a red headband. As the camera flashed, the guy flashed his knife into the air.

"Sai daqui, porra!" he shouted. It meant, Get the f%@# out of here!

The other gang members that ran the area crawled out of the rundown homes and back streets with set jaws and clenched fists.

Teri and I glanced at each other, and without saying a word, we threw the candy away so the hundreds of kids surrounding us would run after it and create a barrier to slow the enemy's approach, giving us a chance to run. My heart is pounding as I write these words, for it was dangerous.

I called Chris Belknap in Hawaii on June 13th to confirm his concert was ready to join with the energy of our team in Rio for the closing ceremony of the *Earth Summit*. I will never forget the feeling I had as the music opened my heart to the rising symphony of goodwill on the planet. My friends Franko Richmond and Gail Lima debuted the song they had written for the occasion, The Time

Has Come. Franko played the piano and Gail led a choir of Brazilian street kids in the chorus.

We were standing beside the stage, and as they began, Teri squealed in delight, "Esmeralda!"

After our big escape, we never thought she would make it, but there she was with about ten of the kids we met in the favelas. I gave her a quick hug, and urged all of them to join the other children on stage as Gail led with the words, "The time has come to love our Earth …"

Standing there in the setting sun as tremendous applause broke out, my eyes filled with tears of happiness. That moment will remain forever embedded in my heart. To top it off, one of my favorite people in the world, Joseph Golden, showed up, freshly arrived from Moscow. I had no idea how he found the resources to get there. The sun glinted off his jacket that was a map of the world. Joseph had taught me music can move consciousness and now I experienced it.

When we finally established the connection with Honolulu, Chris Belknap, who was running the Campaign for the Earth, Hawaii and his guests were singing The Time Has Come as well.

At that moment, thousands of us were alive with the resolution to work together to create a world that respected our environment, the animals and the diversity of human life. The kids sang the chorus again with crystalline voices.

THE TIME HAS COME
To love our Earth
She is our home
She gave us birth
THE TIME HAS COME
To clean the seas
To clear the air
To save the trees
If we listen to our hearts
We can make another start
Then we can find the hope
And find the strength

> To dream again, to dream...
> If we see the world as whole
> And we share a common goal
> Maybe it's not too late
> To heal the wounds
> And celebrate!
> **THE TIME IS HERE**

Years later, Dave and I played that song at our wedding. But back in Rio, we had no clue about that. I liked him, but he was too intellectual, not really interested in spiritual matters, and more into science than I was. He saw me as an airy fairy flight attendant with New Age ideas who didn't even fully understand the concept of ozone depletion.

Joseph and I hugged after the concert and he said something that would change the direction of my life.

"This is the energy; this is the energy that will change the world!" he said with authority in his powerful Russian accent.

"Nancy, now is the time for YOU to join the momentum. Move to New York. Think about it! You can still work as a flight attendant and spend every day off at the United Nations! This will lead you to your destiny!"

In a moment, I knew he was right. All I wanted was to use my fleeting life to make an impact and help raise the consciousness of humanity. I had to do this. Rolling Thunder never really materialized, and I didn't even see Rennie and Sasha at the concert. It didn't really matter. I knew what I had to do.

I was in a dream at the airport the next day, excited about embarking on the next chapter in my destiny. The flight to San Francisco was leaving the next gate over. I saw a nice-looking ash-blond guy talking on his phone. I walked a little closer to be sure I was not mistaking him for somebody else.

"Hey, Dave, is that you?" I asked.

He put down the phone and gave me a brief hug that sent an electric energy pulse through my body.

"Ready to go home?"

Years later...

"Yes. I mean, no. I'm moving to New York!" I blurted out. "It's a big switch from Hawaii and Boulder, but I can request a transfer and still work as a flight attendant and spend every day at the UN to be a part of this amazing new energy!"

He looked at me, and a gigantic smile broke out on his face.

"That is a fabulous idea. You must do it!"

I could see the sparkles around his head again.

We promised each other to stay in touch and exchanged phone numbers. Although I liked him so much, I did not think of him romantically, but knew I had made a friend for life. To this day, time stands proof I was right.

CHAPTER 5
NEW YORK, NEW YORK!

With my team at our United Nations press conference

AMERICAN AIRLINES APPROVED my transfer request to New York sooner than I expected. I took it as a good omen, having no clue it was going to be so different from every place I had experienced so far.

For a few years, starting in 1992, I became a city girl. Picture a Californian girl used to waking up to the pounding of the surf and the cerulean blue of the sky, always wearing airy dresses and flip-flops and driving everywhere, trying to get a cab on Fifth Avenue or finding her way in the subway maze in three-inch heels. It could be scary.

The only way for us to grow as human beings is to leave our comfort zones. Although the beginning may seem smooth and secure, we need to take a deep breath and brace ourselves for the challenges ahead. New York had always intrigued me as being a center of power, but if not for the United Nations, I would never have chosen to live there. The first bite of the Big Apple as a resident tasted bitter, though. Brooke, a dear friend of mine, had invited me to stay over until I got my own place. She had a cool apartment in the Upper East side, close to Madison Avenue.

To save money, I took the bus from the airport to her place—just me, the hope in my heart, the determination in my mind, and one suitcase. I sat in the worn-out navy vinyl seat by the window and wrapped my magenta pashmina around my shoulders. (New York can be cool as fall.)

As the bus ventured on the busy streets, more people got in—some wearing business outfits, others shabby clothes—as if the city wanted to give me a preview of what was to come. About halfway to my destination, a white guy with strands of silver hair sprinkled in his chestnut beard asked for permission to sit next to me. He didn't really have to, so I appreciated that and said, yes. I had also noticed the peace sign on the white T-shirt he was wearing underneath an unbuttoned checkered shirt.

"First day in New York?" he asked after a while. I nodded yes and smiled.

"Hi, my name's Rich," he continued in a slightly nasal voice, as if he had a cold.

"Nancy!" I extended my right hand. He felt rough, and for a second, I pictured him at the dock, unloading ships.

"What brings you here, Nancy?"

Still fresh from my year in Hawaii, my wide-open heart was like a sponge—ready to take whatever God had in store for me.

"I believe people can travel and help other people. Especially us, flight attendants. I'm moving to Manhattan to represent the Campaign for the Earth at the United Nations and explore how we can do that. American Airlines covers my basic bills, but we need money to at least cover our travel expenses..." I replied.

His faded-blue eyes suddenly livened up and, although the bus was noisy with New York's bustle and hustle and nobody was looking at us, he leaned close to my ear.

"I can help you. I can help you a lot!" he whispered.

"Really?"

Rich winked and his bright smile revealed two rows of strong white teeth as he struck his right hand over his heart.

"I promise you! How much money do you have?"

"Not much. About $500 in savings..."

"That's enough." Enough for what, I should have asked myself. "I can triple that for you in no time."

In the next five minutes, Rich convinced me to get off the bus next to the nearest bank, withdraw my savings, and give it to him. Once the five $100 bills disappeared in his shirt pocket, he promised he would return the money to Brooke's address, which I had scribbled on a piece of paper I had ripped off my journal.

"See you on Tuesday and thanks so much!"

"Of course, see you then with at least $1,500!"

As I watched Rich picking up his pace and throwing quick glances over his shoulder, a lump in my throat warned me I would never see him again. For a moment, the quarrel in my mind —*You should stop him!* versus *Don't get paranoid; you need to have faith!* — suffused the voice of my heart, and I suddenly felt exhausted. All I wanted was to hug my dear friend, take a long hot bath, and lay down.

Brooke lived in the apartment her mom left to her. It was huge by New York standards with many antiques, and a plush sofa, slip-covered with a cheery Kelly green and white Laura Ashley print. Like most apartments in the Big Apple, appliances were old.

Brooke and I met in Costa Rica at the Seeking the True Meaning of Peace conference with the inspirational former UN Under Secretary General, Robert Mueller, before I went to Hawaii. We hit it off instantly because of our shared interest in Alice Bailey's writings and serving humanity. She was about my age, 39, and a gorgeous, honey-colored blond. A former Vice President at Chase Morgan and coordinator of the First Earth Run, my friend was now working with United Earth running the Foundation for Claes Nobel of the Nobel Peace Prize family. A true New Yorker, she didn't cook or drive. My mother had kept me out of the kitchen, but I had ended up loving cooking. Jim had contributed to my passion for the creative part of making tasty food. At the end of a long day in New York, I missed his loving embrace, his firm body spooning mine. I guess, despite my busy schedule, part of me missed just being in a relationship. Sometimes I tried to use the kitchen appliances to cook a meal like Jim and I used to, but it wasn't the same.

Rich never showed up, nor did he send the money. I had to ask for Brooke's help until my next paycheck and use public transportation to get around. Often, as I walked in the streets or rode in the filthy subway, I dreamed, my eyes wide open, of being at "Secret Spot", my special vantage spot atop the ocean cliffs in La Jolla or sitting on the beach on North Shore Oahu. It was my way of escaping the smell of urine and the dirt and the begging hands asking for a dime, food, and, sometimes, a joint. Ignoring those hands saddened me the most, for I wanted to help the homeless. However, as soon as I gave money to one person, 20 more people begged me and I could only help so many from my flight attendant salary. My aura was naturally open, but I realized if I wanted to survive in New York and fulfill my mission, I had to close myself down. I took a part-time job with Brooke, helping her with a big event for United Earth to make some extra money to replace the funds I kept giving away.

The first day I stepped inside the UN headquarters in New York in an official capacity, everything looked fascinating as if I had a set of new eyes – the House of Micah (from Hopi prophecy) rising 39 floors into the air; the Diplomatic Entrance lined by the flags of 139 nations; the sculptures outside the entrance, the knotted gun, as a symbol of nonviolence and bronze; the world outside the UN Entrance; Marc Chagall stained glass window on the west side of the lobby; the massive pendulum outside the General Assembly hanging from the 75-foot ceiling. I was grateful for the opportunity to be working alongside the UN Goodwill Ambassadors and other prominent personalities who volunteered their time, talent, and passion to improve the lives of billions of people.

As a registered UN Representative for the Campaign for the Earth, I was allowed to attend the weekly briefings for NGOs and other important meetings. I learned as much as I could, attended meetings, and never missed a chance to share my vision for Airline Ambassadors International and get people's feedback.

Richard Jordan, who I had met during the Earth Summit Preparatory Conference, became my guide. He was a fountainhead of knowledge, familiar with intricacies of UN policies and a true mentor. I loved having lunch with him in the UN Cafeteria, with glass windows overlooking the beautiful Hudson River. Smart and open-minded people would join the table for inspiring discussions of how to cooperate, collaborate and move the world to a sustainable future. I loved to share these conversations with my new friend, Dave Rivard. We stayed in touch, exchanging letters and talking on the phone, and he was always eager to know whom I met and what I learned.

In January of 1993, I took a little break from New York. My friends Elisabet Sahtouris and Diane Sherwood invited me to attend Bill Clinton's Inauguration, on January 20th. I couldn't miss this historic opportunity and promptly accepted not knowing I was in for another big change in my life. Before I go on, let me share a bit about my friends.

I first heard Elisabet speak at a conference in Costa Rica. Author of "Gaia's Dance," she was by far one of the most articulate people I knew on the topic of Earth being a living system. Later on, I introduced her on stage at our Campaign for the Earth events in Rio. Bottom line, I worshiped her. To give you an idea of the type of person she was, when working on her PhD in biology, she moved to Greece and married a Greek fisherman 15 years her junior. She would spend her days rowing in the Mediterranean pondering how to explain living systems to children; by night she cooked for her husband and his fisherman friends. She was brilliant, spontaneous, wild and tons of fun as well as a fabulous networker.

Diane and I had met at one of the preparatory meetings for the Earth Summit; we connected more on the spiritual level. She was another stellar intellect, had a huge heart, and was active in the interfaith movement. She lived in Washington, DC and represented the famed economist Hazel Hendersen.

Elisabet and Diane had visited with me in New York a few months earlier helping with writing promotional material for a concept paper for Airlines Ambassadors International. Both encouraged me to keep pushing the airlines in the right direction.

The three of us volunteered to help at the Homeless Presidential Inaugural Ball— Diane had pulled some strings and got passes so that we could attend any of the ten Inaugural Balls, taking place all over the city. I was bubbling with excitement thinking I'd be in the same room with Vice President, Al Gore, whom I adored and who also wrote one of my favorite non-fiction books, "Earth in the Balance: Ecology and the Human Spirit."

The inauguration celebration lasted for five days and involved an open house at the White House and numerous street festivities, a mixture of Woodstock and MTV. Inclusion—the theme of the event—resonated with me and my vision for bringing love into action, unity and focusing on what unites us.

I fell in love with Washington right away. People were friendlier than New Yorkers, greeting me in the street even though they didn't know me; the DC Metro, clean and efficient, was a pleasure to ride; and the Washington Monument, centered in a perfect cross on the National Mall, served as inspiration to all who visited this city built on the values of democracy and freedom (as opposed to the focus on capitalism so pervasive in New York).

On top of it, I could almost touch the joy and thrill buzzing in the air like a magnetic charge of hopes for a better future and the high expectations built around this young and handsome president. The older generation remembered J.F. Kennedy, and we hoped the new president would love America and its people and stand up for it as much as his illustrious predecessor. Elisabet felt it too; we both wanted to be part of that buzzing energy. My three days in

Washington went by in the blink of an eye. When I left, I fantasized about moving to Washington D.C.

Back in New York, I found comfort in my tiny apartment. I had eventually rented a place of my own, closer to the UN headquarters, on 67th Street and Lexington Avenue. The owner, my friend Lili, lovingly called it the "Lili Pad". Nestled on the third floor at the end of two narrow flights of stairs, the tiny but darling one-bedroom loft exuded a special and magical energy. It was all in pink and green with a cozy little kitchen. A small couch sat across from a padded alcove that looked like something out of a Moroccan dream. There were many nooks for my candles and esoteric spiritual books.

Shortly after I moved in, my friends—old and new — started coming to see me often, as if drawn by an invisible magnet. One time, there were six to seven people crammed into my living room and kitchen. I guess positive energy is contagious and those who can't get it straight from the source get it from people who have it. I loved entertaining, meaningful conversations, laughing, and dancing. But in my heart of hearts, I wanted to be alone.

It took me a while to face the truth and accept what was going on. Although it was exciting to be in New York, not only were the people in the street pulling on me, but my friends were pulling on me too—it seemed that everyone wanted some of my energy.

Mother came to visit for a few days, which I thought would be fun, but when I proudly invited her to see the United Nations, she said she wasn't the least bit interested. I had hoped she would be proud of me for following my intuition and wanting to do something significant with my life, but the truth was even she had no idea who I really was. After Mom left I felt depressed for the first time in my life. There was emptiness inside me, a loss of connection.

I didn't have a boyfriend.

I felt lonely, a hole inside me, a lack of everything.

I didn't realize I needed alone time. I wanted to stay positive and say yes to everyone who asked something of me, but I was resisting listening to the voice in my heart.

On the frosty morning of February 14, 1993 (Valentine's Day), I began my morning meditation. Normally, when I meditate, I feel the down-pouring love of the Shabda current, filling my body with energy and my heart with joy. Only this time when I went inside there was nothing. Zero! I felt nothing at all. This had never happened before. I panicked.

What's going on?

My heart whispered,

"Surrender, surrender, surrender. Feel the emptiness. Be here now."

But what was this emptiness? Since my childhood, I had always been able to still myself and turn my consciousness upward to receive down pouring energy, almost like taking a shower. I had never understood what people were talking about with depression. But now I did, and it was horrible — the emptiness, despair, hopelessness. Now I could understand and have compassion for those who were driven to suicide.

Be here now...

If I couldn't feel the love and joy, maybe this was God's will too? Maybe I was supposed to surrender that which was most precious to me, the inner connection. I surrendered as best I could, trying to accept I was going through this for a reason, but the emptiness stayed with me like a hole in my heart.

A few hours later, American Airlines informed me I was assigned to a flight to Rio de Janeiro. It happened often to be on a schedule and to get a call to replace someone who was suddenly unavailable. I needed the money and wanted to get away from New York to a city that held many wonderful memories for me.

Three hours into the flight, four chimes rang throughout the cabin.

1, 2, 3, 4....

In all my years of flying, I had never experienced four chimes, the signal for an in-flight emergency. My heart racing, my palms sweaty, I looked at Myrna, the youngest flight attendant on board.

Her eyes were wide open, her pupils dilated. She confirmed with a nod the accuracy of my auditory sense. Four chimes signal an in-flight Emergency.

The purser went immediately to the cockpit. He came out a few minutes later and gathered all ten flight attendants in the back galley. His voice was steady, yet I noticed a vein throbbing at his neck. He pulled out a cigarette and lit it (in those days you could still smoke on airplanes).

"We've lost an engine, we're going down into the Atlantic. We've got to prepare for an emergency ditching. Get your manuals."

You don't want to know how thick those red manuals were or how the mind's wheels fast-rewind for the information you learned during your flight-attendant training, hoping you'd never need it. We were supposed to remember everything — what to do, what commands to yell at people, how to get the rafts out in case we'd survive. But with a ditching, you usually wouldn't.

We didn't tell passengers they might die. We told them we had an emergency and needed to collect their shoes for their safety. Some passengers, especially the older ones, clung to their shoes for a second before letting them go from their hands. I could sense their fear. However, I sensed no fear from the five Buddhist monks on board. They handed their sandals to me with a slight bow of their heads and a smile, as if amused by a good joke. When you're connected to Source, the fear of death is but a joke.

I went to the bathroom, looked deeply into my own eyes in the mirror, and whispered, "Beloved God, this morning I got the message from you to surrender. If necessary, I will surrender my life. I don't think I've finished my work and am supposed to die yet, but if it's Your will to take my body, I surrender it to You. Let me save as many people as I can and help me remember what I need to do".

About 10 minutes later, the purser gathered us again and shared that the pilots had decided to turn the plane around, dump fuel, and attempt a landing in San Juan, Puerto Rico. In a way, we were relieved and prayed this wouldn't be our last landing.

As we made our way back, strong turbulence struck the plane, tossing it like a toy in a hurricane, as if trying to test our faith and the aircraft's resistance to severe weather. I was flight attendant

#6 and my jump seat was in the middle of the plane, facing the passenger seats. Everyone was staring at me, their faces livid with terror, clenched jaws. Infants were screaming, and I wished I could calm them.

However, the Buddhist monks, their hands joined in prayer in front of their hearts, radiated peace and love. I tried, too, to radiate peace as the plane hit the ground with a huge bump and bang, and several people screamed. The monks remained relaxed until slowly, despite strong turbulence, the aircraft safely came to a stop on the runway in San Juan. Nobody was harmed, and the whole plane broke out in applause.

I breathed a sigh of relief as I looked at the emergency fire trucks outside. They had parked us away from the populated areas (in case there had been a crash). Over the PA, the Captain reassured the 157 passengers that they could deplane normally and would be bussed to the airport where agents would meet them and route them back to Rio de Janeiro. He instructed the flight attendants to prepare for arrival. I stood by my jump seat to say goodbye to each passenger and, as the monks filed by, I locked eyes with each of them, my hands together in the traditional gesture of Namaste. I swear I saw their eyes twinkling, and though I will never know for sure, they must have had something to do with our miraculous landing.

Airport officials acted distracted and nobody showed any interest in the pilots and cabin crew, although it was traumatic to expect death and then act as if nothing happened. The pilots and purser informed us that AA was deadheading our crew (riding as passengers) back to New York on the next flight.

It took American Airlines another five days to call and ask me if I needed counseling. By that time, any negative emotions, including depression and emptiness, were long gone. My willingness to deeply surrender to the Divine Plan, even my own life if need be, was what allowed me to open up again to the magic of the present moment. After almost dying, the energy came in again in my morning meditations. After all, I had been born a second time.

I found the strength to say *no* to my friends when I needed time alone and embraced being single. I left places, situations, and people that were holding me back even when my heart was torn into pieces. I also doubled the time I was spending at the UN headquarters.

One month later, in March of 1993, the President of the former Soviet Union, Mikhail Gorbachev, launched the Green Cross, an NGO for the environment, in Kyoto, Japan. I had run into him one time at the UN, when I was late for the NGO briefings. I worshiped him; in my spiritual search days in Russia, I used to read his speeches and was so inspired. My friend, Hugh Locke, who was coordinating the Green Cross conference, invited me to take part as a volunteer. I was overjoyed thinking this was the best thing that had ever happened to me—Gorbachev, the Prime-Minister of Japan, David Suzuki, editors of Time and Newsweek, and other brilliant thinkers, would all be attending. Also, I envisioned flight attendants making a positive impact in the world by volunteering at international events and being exposed to global ideas for building a sustainable future.

I was so excited that I wrote another proposal to American Airlines and, this time, United Airlines. Plus, every time I worked a trip, I couldn't help but bubble over with excitement to the other flight attendants I was volunteering at the launch of the Green Cross by Mikhail Gorbachev, the global leader who had just left office in early 1991.

"It will be so exciting to spend time with so many leading edge thinkers!" I was telling them. "We just need to cover our own travel and expenses, but the opportunity is one in a lifetime!"

But they rolled their eyes as I shared, not in the least bit interested in building a better world or in any of my ideas, and went on talking about their boyfriends. One said, "Sure, I'll go if you can get my expenses paid and I could stop off in Korea to go shopping in E Tae Won!"

The airlines didn't get it either. I received zero response from my letters and phone calls. After my last follow-up call to Henry Joyner's office at American Airlines where they flat out told me they were not interested, I was extremely discouraged.

I sat on my special meditation pillow in the Lili Pad, surrounded by candles. As the light flickered off the light green and pink tapestries, I asked for guidance.

How am I going to do it? How am I going to have any influence on the travel industry, one of the largest industries in the world? No one is the least bit interested in any of my ideas. Not airlines, not flight attendants!

I listened intently to the inner silence as the warm Shabda Current filled my body with warmth.

"*Master, what am I to do?*" I asked again... At first, there was nothing, but then I heard a voice deep inside my heart.

Stop talking about it and start doing it.

"*What do you mean?*" I knew people didn't learn from talking, they learned from experiences. The voice came again, almost audible:

"*Stop talking about it, start doing it, and watch what happens.*"

I could do that. People need an example; I might as well be the one. I don't really care about what others think of me. I do care about following the voice inside me."

That March morning of 1993, I made a pivotal decision that changed the direction of my life. I decided I would take one action a month to directly help a child, the Earth or humanity. I would do it myself and follow the yellow brick road as it unfolded in front of me.

The action in front of me was the invitation to help at the launch of the Green Cross in Kyoto, Japan, the following month. I finished my meditation on a high and called Hugh Locke to let him know he could count on me for Kyoto.

CHAPTER 6
BEGINNINGS AND ENDINGS

My first encounter with Mikhail Gorbachev, 1993

BEFORE MOVING FORWARD with my story, I need to give you a little background. I heard Rama Vernon speak in San Diego in 1989 and learned of her desire to ease tensions between the United States and the former Soviet Union. I connected with her as a yoga teacher, and joined her trip organized by Center for International Dialogue to act as a "Citizen Diplomat." On that trip, I met Joseph Golden. He had helped with the Space Bridge between Moscow and San Bernardino, CA in 1982. We later became great friends (and he inspired me to create a primitive space bridge at the Hawaii Youth Summit). I read Gorbachev's inspiring speeches which were distributed all over Moscow and Leningrad and believed him to be one of the great luminaries of our time. His speeches were based on an understanding that all humanity was connected with one another and the Earth. It would be so amazing to actually meet this man!

The Global Forum for Spiritual and Parliamentary Leaders of Human Survival took place every five years, and, at this meeting, Mikhail Gorbachev was launching the Green Cross! What an incredible opportunity! This conference would have the flavor of a Wisdom Keepers gathering as it drew statesmen and spiritual leaders of all faith traditions.

Determined to stay true to my inner promise, in April 1993, I got on the plane to Kyoto, thus embarking on my first mission, the lone Airline Ambassador. My friend Nina, representing her organization - Children of the Earth, joined me. Sadly, I could not inspire any other flight attendants to participate.

The theme of the conference was "Value Change for Global Survival." Nearly 500 delegates from dozens of countries attended. The world's most potent spiritual, parliamentary, and scientific minds gathered to engage in reflections on humanity's survival and how to live more sanely on a small planet awakening from a greed to green mentality. It was incredible.

The religious tapestry was dizzying—Muslims in snow white linen; Shinto priests in woven silk robes; Buddhists in elegant ochre; the Hindu delegate, renowned statesman Dr. Karan Singh in fine linen kurta; religious leaders, Dadi Janki, and J.P. Vaswani in soft white robes; political giants such as Mikhail Gorbachev in dapper business suits; Native American Indians bedecked with sacred stone pendants; full-bearded rabbis in black; regal-looking Russian Orthodox priests with hooded caps; an Italian Franciscan monk in a brown habit; and Africans in bright, embroidered garb, all gathered in the dramatic oriental charm of Kyoto, Japan's cultural jewel.

Upon our arrival, Nina and I were exhausted after our long flight, but still joined Hugh Locke's meeting for volunteers. Bawa Jain was also a volunteer – (we had met at the Wisdom Keepers in Rio as he was assistant to the Realized Master, Sushil Kumar, head of the Jain sect – affectionately called Guruji). We hugged and when I asked if Guruji was there, Bawa assured me he was OK but could not be in Kyoto for this meeting. There were only fourteen of us, and Hugh explained that each day there would be 14 break out groups after the Plenary. He assigned each of us different venues to take notes and make sure we captured the essence of each conversation. I was thrilled with this assignment and all the interesting people around me.

I couldn't take my eyes off these two guys from Estonia, about 6' tall—they were so magnetic. One had his head shaved and the other had sandy hair. They seemed to be in their 30s and were very buff with strong physiques. It turned out they studied with shamans in their country. Who knew shamans lived in a place as remote as Estonia? It would be fun to meet each afternoon with the sexy guys, Aleksei and Kristofer!

After the meeting for volunteers, we joined the international welcome dinner in the Sakura Room, where we were served dishes of sweet/sour pickled radish, sashimi, green tea and sake on tatami mats. I had to pinch myself with excitement as we tucked in under beautifully patterned futon quilts.

The General Secretary of the United Nations, Boutros Boutros Ghali, sent his message for the opening ceremony: "The issues of the international community that once seemed so different—economic democracy, peace and security and sustainable development – we now know are part of the same human endeavor."

When Mikhail Gorbachev got up to speak, I was near the podium. Luckily, I was wearing my red suit. I always feel more powerful when I wear red and deep down in my soul, I instinctively knew Gorbachev would resonate with this color. Although he spoke in Russian through translators, I felt his spirit and its almost palpable power. He was glad to launch the International Green Cross, a global, non-governmental agency dedicated to protecting the defenseless endangered life forms—plants and animals—being erased from the planet due to economics and destructive technologies. School children had welcomed him with a song when he first arrived in Kyoto and he ended his speech with that.

"Their song: Dear Mother, Mother Earth, gives me hope that our children will lead us in the value change which is so necessary if we are to save our Earth."

The 500 delegates stood to clap for him in the Plenary Hall, and what a show of unity it was. While still clapping, Bawa came up to me and offered to introduce me to this great man. He ushered me to the left so I could be there when Gorbachev exited the stage. Sure enough, Bawa introduced us.

"Mr. Gorbachev, it is such an honor to meet you," I exclaimed, my heart pounding with excitement. "I am working with flight attendants around the world to enlist support in environmental and humanitarian agendas. Our group will be called Airline Ambassadors International." As I spoke, a tall Russian translator translated my words into his ear. Gorbachev looked me straight in the eye and replied with a thick accent, "Very good, very good!"

He then reached out to shake my hand. His touch was firm, yet gentle. I wished Joyner from American Airlines was there to see me and hear how a renowned global leader was acknowledging my ideas. Bawa snapped a picture of Gorbachev and me; I still have it and keep it in my special photo album.

For four days, discussions circumnavigated the globe, putting environmental and social problems under scrutiny so all could see the need for greater cooperation. Dr. Karan Singh was among the most eloquent speakers, but there were many others who challenged big-business callousness. Dada JP Vaswani emphasized that we must recognize there is one life that flowers into all; Phil Lane, Chief of the Dakota, highlighted indigenous peoples that have preserved the sacred relationship with our sacred Mother Earth.

"You must forgive us, Lord, for being unkind not only to one another but to the whole of Creation because we did not look at the sun as Brother Sun, the Earth as Mother and Sister Earth, the sea as Brother and Sister Sea," a Franciscan man prayed, bringing tears to my eyes.

On our last night, my friend Nina, some of the other volunteers, and I agreed to enjoy a Japanese bath.

There were 14 of us, seven women and seven men, and the baths were separated by gender. We got in a series of baths with water of different temperatures. I asked for a towel to wrap around my body, but all they gave me was a tiny washcloth. I hesitated–exposing my naked body in front of strangers wasn't something I'd typically do. I also remembered how, for centuries, we have been conditioned to be ashamed of our bodies or, at least, some very specific parts of it when, in reality, there is nothing to be embarrassed about. The human body is a beautiful and perfect creation of God and fully worthy of love.

My cheeks flushed as I decided to take the challenge and be no-body and followed the other women into the first bath. Still self-conscious, I plunged into the clear water. At first, we didn't really look at each other, pretending relaxation was more important than bonding. But slowly and surely, our tongues loosened, chatting and bantering until we forgot about our nudity. At the end of the 7th bath, everybody felt truly exhilarated. We went out to greet the men and sat beside the river with trees full of cherry blossoms that seemed to glisten in the light of the full moon overhead. Suddenly, the mesmerizing, soulful sound of a Shakuhachi (a traditional Japanese bamboo flute), rang out in that magical light. It was Masakazu Yoshizawa, the famous flutist, who was also at the conference. What a joy to share his songs in the moonlight; I only wished Dave could have been there.

I had booked my way home the following day after the closing ceremony of the Forum through Honolulu with a four-hour interval, just enough time to get to the North Shore. I loved being in New York, but I missed having romance in my life. I also missed Jim, and part of me needed closure. I rented a car and drove straight to Jake's Restaurant in Haleiwa.

As I entered the familiar entrance with plastic glowing flowers on the entry table, it turned out my intuition had been right. Jim was tending at the bar looking as gorgeous as ever with his faded rayon Hawaiian shirt and long wispy ponytail curling over his left shoulder. He sensed my presence immediately and our eyes met.

"Nancy, what are you doing here?" he exclaimed, his face lit by a gigantic smile.

"Hi, Jim! I went to the most amazing conference in Kyoto, and I'm only here on a short layover. Is there any way you can take a break? I can't stay long…"

"Sure, it's not too busy. Give me five minutes, and we can take a walk …"

I waited for him, my heart pounding. Then we walked out arm-in-arm to that same full moon that shone down on us the night before in Kyoto and sat in the sand, under palm trees, gazing at each other for a while. I was the first one to break the silence, eager to share with him the significance of the Global Forum and how my life had changed in New York, and the joy of being a part of history. Jim listened politely and when I was done talking, he gave me a long and gentle kiss.

And with that, my last ounce of hope we could still be together died away. It was easy to notice Jim had no interest. He was still the same guy, content with surfing and bartending, and that would never change. The realization hit me hard and soon it was time to get back to my flight, I had to leave.

He walked me to the car, and I blew him a kiss out the window. I knew now we weren't a good match, and I had made the right decision in leaving him, yet bitter tears rolled down my cheeks all the way to the airport and most of the flight back to New York. What had I done? The deep poignancy of the moment grabbed me as I had given up temporal happiness with Jim…for what? An elusive mission that may not even manifest?

The truth was I was lonely and longed for connection. I remembered my visit to Sai Baba in India, when I asked him if I should marry. He emphatically said not to marry the man I was with, but counseled me to wait.

"Better one coming!" he clearly told me.

When was that better one ever going to come?

I knew for sure I had to move forward, towards my Mission.

A few days later, Elisabet Sahtouris invited me to move to Washington, DC. She had found two studio apartments in Washington, DC, a few blocks from the White House and walking distance from the National Mall. She argued that we could both have our own space but be in the same building. Inspired by the vote of confidence from Gorbachev, I took this as a sign from God and said YES!

The apartment was only $700 per month, half of what I was paying in New York. I didn't need a car, and could commute by metro to the airport. The DCA flight attendant base at American Airlines base was not open, but a benefit of being a flight attendant is that you can commute. I put in a transfer request to Miami and it went through immediately! I moved to Washington DC on August 1, 1993.

At our first dinner together, Elisabet told me about the Prayer Vigil for the Earth, coming up in October. Her friend, Sharon Franquemont, had a vision about this and inspired Grandfather Harry Bird, (Lakota), Grace Smith Yellowhammer (Diné), Betsy Stang, and David Berry helped organize a special event. The One Mind, One Voice, One Heart, One Prayer Vigil was scheduled to be held on the National Mall. This 30-hour prayer marathon was meant for Native Wisdom Keepers to heal national wounds and bring respect to spirituality. Thomas Banyaca (who I had met on the Hopi Reservation in 1981) was to be one of the elders participating. Since there weren't enough hotel room for all the participants, Elisabet and I offered our places.

I was honored to give my apartment to Thomas Banyaca (I met him on the Hopi Reservation and witnessed him revealing the Hopi Prophecy at the UN in 1992). Elisabet put all 14 Grandmothers on floor mats in her apartment. When I told my dear friend Annette Lantos, (wife of Congressman Tom Lantos), she offered to host the Grandmothers to lunch in a private Congressional Dining Room. It was amazing and Annette, the perfect hostess, got all the Grandmothers smiling and talking about their children.

Thousands of people came to the Mall, admired the tipis, and talked to the elders. The Peace Pipe Ceremony brought together people of all races, ages, and political beliefs. (I didn't know then I would have a pipe ceremony at my own wedding). The Prayer Vigil offered this precious gift to Washington, DC giving the example of peace and tolerance of all.

October wasn't all happiness. American Airlines turned me down when I asked for tickets as a prize for the year's UN Youth Competition with the NGO Paz y Cooperacion. I couldn't stand another rejection so, in a moment of weakness and devoid of the support of my family or a loving partner, I almost gave up.

Dear Father, I don't want this mission anymore. Please, take it from me, I sat in meditation and prayed.

"You don't have to do it, Nancy, if you don't want to. We can give the assignment to somebody else," (I silently breathed a sigh of relief) but then more came: "But you CAN do it. You ARE prepared."

I knew I had to, at least, TRY!

So I grit my teeth and decided to bite the bullet. I bought my first computer and got back to it. I tweaked my one-page document outlining the intended objectives of Airline Ambassadors International. Pleased with the new result, I sent it to Dave Rivard. I trusted and respected his experience as an environmentalist and head of the California World Foundation. He thought it was great and said, "Nancy, you are going in the right direction, Keep it up!"

In retrospect, Dave was my biggest supporter since the day we met. A divine blessing in my life, he was always there for me at the right time, and helped me remain focused on my mission. We wouldn't meet in person for months, yet when it happened, we'd pick right where we'd left off as if we said good-bye the day before. The friendship and trust we had built before we became romantically involved and our inner growth created a strong foundation for our marriage, which lasts to this day.

For the next 12 months, I adjusted to my new life in Washington, DC. It was such fun to live near my close friends, Elisabet Sahtouris and Diane Sherwood. I met with Annette Lantos almost weekly at her husband's Congressional Office and even helped at her events. Both Annette and her husband had fled Hungary when Hitler was still in power. Theirs was the kind of special union that fairy tales are made of, and one that I wanted to eventually have if only I'd meet the right man! In high school, I wrote this poem:"*Each to each our first love, not the other but the Sun,*

Only then our hearts can beat together two as One."

But I'd learned to be patient and trust the divine timing to find my destined mate and work together on a mission bigger than ourselves.

CHAPTER 7
THE ONE REVEALED

Dave and I joining our visions and forces

I ATTENDED THE 50th Anniversary of the signing of the UN Charter in San Francisco, and Dave Rivard invited me to stay a few more days at his ranch. It was actually a huge dome located in Half Moon Bay that sat on 80 acres in a pocket of pristine open space with deer and wildlife all around.

Dave warned me I might see mountain lions in the driveway and golden eagles nesting in the yard. I couldn't wait to see it and agreed. As Dave gave me the tour, I realized the ranch was everything he promised and beyond. Dave had built himself a breathtaking white dome, with a totally open floor plan with lots of light. A ladder led up to a loft where there was a big comfy bed and an adjoining bathroom.

A small fireplace, a low maple burl table, and a couple chairs decorated the open plan. On the far side was a magnificent large dining table and a large airy kitchen in the back to the left. He had hundreds of books on his bookshelves on Latin American history, herpetology (the study of reptiles), and microbiology by authors such as Noam Chomsky. Dave pulled out "When Corporations Rule the World," one of the books by Dave Korten and showed me on the jacket where the author had thanked him personally.

For our first dinner, he cooked my childhood favorite—-steak—-on his small grill while I prepared the salad. It felt so natural, as if we were a couple, as if we belonged together. After we finished eating, we shared stories and neither of us ran short.

I started by telling Dave about the little boy I met during my recent trip to Santa Cruz, Bolivia, where I went to a children's hospital. As I stepped inside the cancer ward, he looked me straight in the eye, silently begging me, Help me! You're the only one who can!

There was also another child suffering from diarrhea. His family needed only one dollar to get the diarrhea medicine that would save his life, which I happily supplied. Talking to my friend, I realized the children needed more help than the suitcase full of shoes I had brought for them. You see, unless a miracle happened, the hospital would close soon for lack of medical supplies. I couldn't let it happen, so I prayed for help. It arrived the next day, on my way back to the US. I was the number one flight attendant (working in First Class) and both the Ambassador of Bolivia to the US and the country director of American Airlines were traveling in my cabin. Upon mentioning the hospital situation, they promised that should I get the supplies, they would get them in.

"The question is," I ended my story, "Where do I get those supplies?"

Dave's face lit up.

"I love delivering medical supplies. If you need them for the cancer ward, I have $250,000 worth in my basement and I'll give them to you."

He had worked with an organization called "Acting, Teaching, Caring, Sharing" and used to deliver supplies all the time. He also offered to connect me to Stanford University so I could get unlimited medical supplies. I was so happy I wanted to jump up and down.

It was almost midnight when I listened to Dave's stories and realized how we had traveled different paths leading us to the same realization—-we wanted to do something significant with our lives.

The son of an ironworker, Dave had grown up in Minnesota, the oldest of nine siblings. His family was the opposite of mine, and they had no rules. He grew up like Huckleberry Finn and sometimes would stay outside for days at a time. That is where he gained such an interest in the environment and wildlife, especially reptiles. At 18, Dave became a Recon Marine and served two tours in Vietnam. Upon discharge, he found all eight of his siblings had been abandoned by both mother and father so he set off to change the law in Minnesota and physically adopted his own brothers and sisters.

He succeeded, thus saving his family from disaster. Would I have had the spiritual maturity to have done the same? No way!

That evening, Dave made quite an impression on me with his breadth of experience. He had learned ironwork like his dad, and started his own company, Steel Reinforcing Inc., which was quite successful, but he didn't stop there. He was always growing and trying new things. He worked on both the National Environmental Protection Act and the Endangered Species Act of 1973, studied classical music and microbiology, owned sailboats, started a gym, and ran marathons. He also started the first wellness-based Preferred Provider Organization, (PPO) -Healthquest.

Dave was also an expert kayaker, and when he told me the story of Expedition Chile, getting separated from the group and being picked up by the Presidential yacht, I rolled on the floor laughing my head off. Dave loved to dance and occasionally would do it all night long, like he did in a Quechua bar with the Mayor of La

Paz. His passion was also herpetology, so he funded an alligator farm in Florida and helped deliver animals to their natural habitat in Bolivia. I didn't realize when I met him that he was so wild and adventurous, but that night my opinion changed.

I suddenly noticed things about him that I hadn't noticed prior, like the strong muscles under his shirt. Dave Rivard's rugged good looks began to attract me in a way they hadn't before ...

A week later, we arranged for Karen Walker, an American Airlines flight attendant in San Francisco to meet Dave at the SFO Airport, and check the 40 boxes of supplies for Santa Cruz, Bolivia. Everything went like clockwork; the Ambassador and the American Airlines representative kept their promise, and when I arrived for my flight attendant layover in Santa Cruz, the Base Manager for AA, Rene Osorrio, told me everything was arranged and there was no problem with Customs.

He told our flight attendant team to go to the hotel to rest, as he had arranged a press conference for us at 4:00 p.m. The whole crew, four flight attendants and two pilots, joined me. It was a huge splash, and the top media outlets in Bolivia attended. We were treated like celebrities and magazines and newspapers did great spreads on our story. It was my first big mission, the beginning of my large-scale humanitarian work, and Dave Rivard made it possible! I couldn't wait to see him again.

In October, Dave decided to take a trip to Washington to meet with the Laborers International Union of North America (LIU-NA) and inspire them to support the environmental movement. We were just friends, but I felt a sort of electricity that wasn't there before when we talked on the phone or when I thought about him. Since LIUNA was only two blocks from my apartment, I invited him to stay with me. I only had a pullout couch I used as a bed for myself, so I put him on a mattress on the kitchen floor. He accepted without any comments or complaints.

Dave's trip overlapped with one of the most powerful events in the '90s, The Million Man March.

"Nancy, we need to go to the coordinating meeting before The Million Man March tonight! I met some guys on the bus to DC and everyone's going. We have to join them," Dave said as soon as he arrived. He had landed in Baltimore, taken the metro to Washington, DC, and gotten hung up on the enthusiasm of the people on the trains attending the movement.

Called by Louis Farrakhan, "The Million Man March" was to be held on and around the National Mall. Prominent speakers were scheduled to address the audience, and African American men from across the United States planned to gather in the heart of Washington to "convey to the world a vastly different picture of the black male" and to unite against economic and social plights pulling down the African-American community. Ultimately, ABC-TV-funded researchers at Boston University estimated the crowd size to be about 837,000 participants.

The coordinating meeting took place at the Washington, DC Convention Center. We were the only white people in attendance and sat about five rows back from the stage.

"Nancy, do you have a checkbook in your purse?" Dave inquired when they asked for donations. "If you do, I want to write a check to support this effort, but, no worries, I will pay you back when we get home!"

I brought out my blue checkbook with my maiden name, Nancy Lynn Larson, printed on it and wrote a check for $500,000 and Dave handed the check to the man on stage and, before I knew it, I heard the announcer shouting:

"We've just received a new donation for $500 from Miss Nancy Lynn Larson for The Million Man March!"

Oh no, my Mom was going to see that on TV! She was an arch-Republican, did not really support my humanitarian work, and would be appalled if I supported something like The Million Man March. Luckily, she never saw the TV coverage, and Dave did pay me back when we returned to my apartment.

The next day, we had lunch with Annette Lantos in the Congressional Dining Room. We had a beautiful time joking and discussing serious matters such as the environment and human rights. After our lunch, the three of us walked out of the dining area to a balcony overlooking the entire Washington Mall which was filled with almost 1,000,000 black people.

"All the Congressmen are hiding in their offices because they're afraid of possible riots or bloodshed," Annette said.

"If I were a Member of Congress, I'd be right out there with them," Dave exclaimed.

Dave and I ended up walking arm-in-arm around the Mall, the only white flesh to be spotted within 1,000 yards. We stopped to take in that amazing, historical view. Dave put his arms around my waist from behind as if he were trying to protect me. And protected and secure I felt. I also felt at peace and happy in knowing I was doing what I was supposed to be doing. I was in the right place at the right time, no detours. Dave cracked so many jokes I laughed my head off.

October 15th is one of those days one remembers until their last breath. I mean, we were witnessing history being made. Louis Farrakhan's discourse did not incite violence, but encouraged black men, all men, to take responsibility for their actions, take care of their families, and be a model for others. He was an amazing orator and I was exhilarated!

Yet, when I look back, a tiny detail pops up, endearing and sweet. On our way home, we went to Old Ebbitt Grill, Washington, DC's oldest saloon —or so they say. Presidents Ulysses Grant, Andrew Johnson, Grover Cleveland, and Theodore Roosevelt, took a moment of respite at its stand-around bar. Earlier in the afternoon, Dave's lips were chapped and I shared with him the only lip balm I had. It was green, but I neglected to let him know it would turn your lips rose-pink. When the waiter took our order, he couldn't take his eyes from Dave's ruby lips and could barely stifle a smile. But I didn't care. I was hanging out with the coolest guy on Earth.

Back home, we decided to end the night with a movie and picked Forrest Gump. As the feature film ran on the screen, it dawned on me that Dave was like Forrest Gump. He oozed kindness, and everything he touched turned to gold, and I admired his courage to just be himself. Dave had had his own realization, too.

"Today, when I had my arms around you, I had this strong feeling that you and I are supposed to do something together. Maybe we're supposed to have a baby together or something? The world needs models of a new kind of couple."

It wasn't like a sexual come-on or anything; he was just saying what he felt. I pondered that. We fell asleep on the pullout couch, cradled in each other's arms, and, as I rested in contentment, I began to feel a tingling in my loins. That night, Dave and I made love for the first time.

CHAPTER 8
A BIG
DECISION

Wearing my lucky suit and smile

I WAS IN London, getting ready for my flight back to the US. When you're a flight attendant, regardless of what happens in your private life, you have to look fresh and perfectly groomed: crisp white shirt, styled hair, held back in a chignon, flawless makeup (not excessive, just enough to enhance the features). Yet my hand was trembling and, for the first time in a long time, I couldn't get my rose-colored lipstick right.

I made love with a man who was just my friend, and now I'm pregnant!

My period was late. The pregnancy test flashed two blue lines, and I hadn't taken any precautions—I was in my early forties and didn't believe I could carry a child anymore. What was I supposed to do? Should I pick up the phone and call Dave?

Our morning goodbye after our passionate night of love, crowning our blooming emotional and intellectual connection, had been cut short by pressing matters. I was on an early flight to London, and Dave had to return to San Francisco. I had averted my eyes, gave him a quick peck, and jumped inside the cab. He reciprocated, but without any attempt to get or show more affection. In retrospect, I'm grateful I'm not the nail-biting kind of woman; otherwise, my manicure would have taken a heavy blow on the way to the airport. I knew numerous situations where sex ruined long-lasting friendships, and didn't want that to happen to me, to us.

Despite my fears, Dave and I stayed in touch as if nothing happened. We never alluded to our physical display of affection. Each time I talked to him, I felt happy. One time, I felt surrounded by this cocoon of love, like an altered state of consciousness, and didn't want to let go of that feeling.

You can do this, Nancy! You've done it a million times!

With one movement of hand, the lipstick finally looked perfect on my lips. I would keep the news from Dave until my gynecologist confirmed the pregnancy. I went to the doctor as soon as I got back home and he confirmed I was with child. The baby was due during the Second United Nations Conference on Human Settlements in June 1996.

"I can't be pregnant now. I need to be at the City Summit in Istanbul," I exclaimed.

"Well, there's nothing you can do about it. You are definitely not going to be able to travel next June, unless you elect to have an abortion," the doctor said in a flat voice. "But you are not that kind of person."

He knew my love for children and my efforts to preserve life where others were destroying it. I felt healthy enough, and I had always wanted a child, but emotionally I was a wreck.

I wondered if Dave was the father I wanted for my child. I knew he would be a fabulous father, and when I thought of him my heart welled up in joy, but he didn't fit my picture of a spiritual boyfriend. He always lifted my energy and was totally on my wavelength. Although he was more intellectual than spiritual, it was clear he was a highly-evolved soul. He had taken in all eight of his brothers and sisters and told me he loved that time of his life because he loved being around kids. I would never have had that kind of commitment or responsibility at age 20. It showed what a special person he was.

He was on a job site when I called him.

"You'd better sit down," I said. "I have something to tell you."

Somehow, he already knew, because he asked me right away, "Are you pregnant?"

I remembered his words from a month ago, that we were meant to birth something together, maybe a baby.

"Yes," I said, allowing myself to feel the joy of nurturing new life inside my womb.

Dave didn't make any promises, but a few hours later he was knocking on my door and holding me tight in his arms, tears in his eyes. I could feel that had I wished it, he would never let me go.

When he finally released me, he stared into my eyes.

"I'm so excited about this and ready to go for it. I want to support you in whatever you decide to do, including this child. You are the woman, and most tuned to the Creator's will. I might not be the right man for you, and only you can know that."

I broke into tears and sobbed for a while. How many men would give a woman this kind of answer? It takes a highly-evolved soul and emotionally mature man to allow a woman to make her choice without taking things personally. Yet, I didn't really want a baby right then, but having an abortion felt even worse.

So we decided to spend a couple of days together. The first day, we would pretend we agreed to get married and the next, pretend that we agreed not to, and see which choice resonated more with both of us. On the third day, I was still torn. Airline Ambassadors International was my other baby, newly born, and needed my full attention and nurturing. Was I ready to be a mother to two infants? Dave wasn't interested in spirituality and didn't check all the boxes as a husband. Would I marry him if I kept the baby? It was hard to say.

Fate spared me from having to make a decision. Shortly after, while working an all-nighter flight to London, a stabbing pain in my stomach almost knocked me off my feet. I ran to the airplane bathroom to find myself bleeding profusely. I knew I was having a miscarriage high in the heavens, over what pilots call The Pond, in the mid-Atlantic Ocean.

Part of me was relieved as it took the pressure off. Part of me grieved the loss of the new life growing in my womb. And there was this other part of me, one that has been asleep for a while and loved romance, which was excited about dating Dave for real. Thinking about the way he had handled the whole situation and our enduring friendship, I came to the realization that he always made me happy. He was so different from the men I'd been involved with before in so many aspects.

For example, one time before our first night of love, I flew to San Francisco to see him. Men wined and dined me, but he didn't do any of that. He didn't make breakfast for me in the morning, either, like Jim used to in Hawaii. He took me for a walk, and instead, offered me an orange. Certainly, Dave was a man of action. Perhaps this was exactly what made him fit to be my husband.

Sitting in my jump seat, my legs tight together, I remembered my experience in Sri Lanka a year after Daddy passed away. An image of this little girl, Dinesha, whom I sponsored, flashed in my mind. I sponsored her through Save the Children, had gone to visit her, and bonded with her deeply. Sadly, when the Tamil war broke out in July 1983, Save the Children pulled out of Sri Lanka, and I was never able to communicate with Dinesha again. I made a promise in my heart to help other children like her, and to create a system where people could directly contact and help one another.

Could Dave be the man I could work with to materialize that goal?

I decided to give him a chance and date him for real to find out.

In November 1995, after I miscarried, Dave and I met in New York for the preparatory meeting of the upcoming United Nations Conference on Human Settlements Habitat II. The event (known as the "City Summit") would take place next year in June in Istanbul, Turkey.

Dave's sister arranged for us to stay in a beautiful apartment, and he suggested we throw a reception for our friends, although the place was rather tiny. He invited his friends — famous authors, heads of delegations, the intellectual type. I invited mine —musicians, artists, flight attendants.

As the guests arrived, I feared the evening would turn into a disaster for we had two different crowds. It began rather stiffly, but everybody still remembers that evening as one of the best parties ever. By the time the music and the wine were flowing, 50 people, including the British Ambassador to the US, were sitting on the floor, singing Frank Sinatra's song "Blue Moon." It was obvious that Dave and I were complimentary energies and we were stronger together than we were apart.

Not only had he helped with medical supplies for the kids in Bolivia, but he was also my rock and gave me the unconditional moral and emotional support I needed. He inspired me to follow my gut instinct and pushed me toward my mission.

While in New York, Dave encouraged me to pursue my idea of hosting a meeting of The Wisdom Keepers — the spiritual elders — at the UN Conference in Istanbul similar to the one at the Earth Summit in Rio. I called Hanne Strong, who had organized the first Wisdom Keepers, to see if she would want to help. She was also in New York at the time and loved the idea. She suggested we have a gathering the following day. I was scheduled to fly, but

Dave encouraged me to follow my intuition: this meeting was more important. I loved that about him—-mission was more important than money—-as well as his not wanting to grab the limelight and letting me do this by myself. He did not even join the meeting!

Fifty people showed up at the Millennium Hotel, across from the UN headquarters, and everyone enjoyed refreshments. I paid out of my flight attendant salary to cover the bill of $150.

However, it totally paid off when one businessman who attended offered us a million dollars for the project! I literally could not believe it and had to pinch myself to make sure this was real. Hanne suggested putting my friend, Bawa Jain, as the key organizer of The Wisdom Keepers meeting, as he was in New York and active with the faith community. Bawa gladly accepted. He was the friend who had introduced me to Gorbachev at the Kyoto meeting.

The same November 1995, Airline Ambassadors International was officially born as a non-profit network of airline personnel who give their time as Ambassadors of Goodwill in a worldwide volunteer service. A fellow flight attendant, Eileen Hudnall, and I had been talking about Airline Ambassadors, and her husband was a Texas attorney. He filed the initial paperwork for incorporation in Texas, the headquarters of American Airlines. The founding Board members were me (President), Dave Rivard (VP), Diane Sherwood, (Secretary) and my dear friend and her husband Eileen and Carl Oates as other Board members.

Annette Lantos invited us to have our first Board meeting in Congressman Tom Lantos' office in the Rayburn House Office at the Capitol. As the staff served ginger cookies and iced tea, we talked about how we would spread humanitarian relief throughout the world and help vulnerable children. We decided we would offer three major programs: humanitarian and environmental services, escorting children for needed medical care, and assisting at conferences and special events. With each action, we would bring compassion into action. At the end of our Board meeting, Congressman Lantos added a second statement in the Congressional Record (he had written his first acknowledgment in 1993, when we initially met).

I felt I could fly. Things were going in the right direction, and as the days went by, Dave and I were becoming more romantically involved with each other. I loved writing him messages on beautiful cards. Here are a few:

Beloved, in recognizing you it is as if a veil has been lifted from my heart and some Great Force is pulling me to leave behind the world I know and enter with you into a world wholly new - with unknown possibilities. We know not where the current will take us - the tadpole knows not the frog, nor the caterpillar the butterfly, but somehow I feel blissful in surrender to the Great Tide that is sweeping us together now towards the Mystery - towards a deeper embodiment of Love, I love you!

Let's meet in our dreams, and pledge our souls to one another and the upliftment of all Life. I love you.

I had a wild dream of you last night and our Life is the wildest dream of a lifetime. May all your dreams come true. HAPPY BIRTHDAY! Let's celebrate today with ANYTHING you want to do - LET'S ENJOY! I am so very grateful you are my BEST friend, my lover and my partner in all ways. Thank you for your love and support, which is my strength!

Sweet dreams my darling - I wish I were in your arms tonight!

My darling, I miss not resting in your arms and look forward to swimming in the world's currents together

Dave had been so right. Airline Ambassadors International was my idea, but we birthed it together.

CHAPTER 9
MADE
IN HEAVEN

A picture of love

AS THE LOVE between Dave and me grew stronger, AAI kept growing, and more flight attendants joined our ranks. Our teams went to Honduras, Mexico, and even Romania, but I had to keep my attention on coordinating for the trip to The United Nations

Conference on Human Settlements in Istanbul scheduled for the month of June 1996. Airline Ambassadors International was the only NGO to bring 50 volunteers, all flight attendants except for Dave, who accompanied me. Each NGO could only officially bring five delegates, but my girlfriend, Sharrye Moore, worked with the UN and knew many NGOs who wanted to be represented. Sharrye did them a service by matching volunteers to these slots. Wally N'Dow, the Secretary General, acknowledged our efforts and said: "You're the only NGO that's really doing things." The conference focused on solutions and aimed at devising a Global Plan of Action for development into the 21st century. Our volunteers helped conference organizers and also with hosting the Award Ceremony with Paz y Cooperacion for the "World's Fair of Ideas for Peace" art competition.

The Wisdom Keepers happened, but not the way we hoped. Bawa Jain, who had offered his help to coordinate things in New York, ended up excluding me entirely. Instead of getting upset, as I had my hands full with managing our volunteers, I arranged to get my friends from National Geographic to join us and make a documentary. They were willing to volunteer their time and just needed to cover logistics. When Bawa said there was no funding available to cover their expenses, they decided not to come. I was furious with Bawa for not authorizing this and put a call out to the Universe to bring a filmmaker into my life.

Dave and I were so excited to travel together through London to Istanbul.

When we got off the plane we were surrounded by the scents of spices and Turkish Delight. Electricity was in the air just like in Rio. For the first few days, we booked a hotel in downtown Istanbul that the UN recommended. It was much like any modern hotel in other European cities. As we checked in, I noticed a tall, nice-looking man standing near us. "Are you here for the United Nations City Summit? I asked.

"It's an odd thing," he replied in a low, resonant voice with a slightly English accent. "I've learned to follow my intuition and I received an inner nudge that my services may be needed in Istanbul. The only one I know here is David Lionel, who is documenting the conference and has a whole editing studio set up down the street. I flew in from Hawaii and am exhausted, but open to what the Universe wants."

My heart knew my prayer had been answered, but I just wanted to make sure.

"What do you do?" I asked. "Oh, I am a filmmaker. You may remember the film "Roger Rabbit" that told the story of what happened with the automobile industry in the United States. Roger Watt is my name." He smiled warmly and put his hand out for me to shake.

I liked him immediately.

"Well, you are not going to believe this," I began. "We have been looking for someone just like you to document Wisdom Keepers II. Unfortunately, Mother Teresa could not make it because of her health, but we have many other Wisdom Keepers from all backgrounds, including Waangari Mathai, Dadi Janke and Millard Fuller, Founder of Habitat for Humanity. There is a Welcome Cruise on the Bosphorus tomorrow evening at 6:00 p.m. to welcome them. Why don't you join us at Topkapi Palace?"

He looked at me and his eyes twinkled. Dave and I glanced at each other then gave each other a kiss and hug. The magic was back!

The United Nations Conference on Human Settlements was very similar to Rio in some ways. It gathered Heads of State, national delegations, non-governmental organizations, global businesses, youth, and spiritual leaders. Many of my friends, who were soaring on an upward spiral, making a difference in the world, were there. Our days were full.

Dave was representing the International Federation of Free Trade Unions, of which all trade unions are co-confederate signatories during a pretty insecure time in Turkey. A week earlier the Turkish government had killed seven union workers. I was greeting the arriving flight attendants daily and getting them set up with daily assignments, helping with the Secretary General's Office, with the Youth Summit and more.

I loved Istanbul's vibe and the late-evening cruises down the Bosphorus Strait, the huge waterway that flows near Istanbul. After the first few days, we learned our way around the city and checked out of our modern hotel in favor of a boutique hotel near the Hagia Sophia and the Blue Mosque. As busy as we were, Dave and I were falling more deeply in love every day. One day he shared a dream that Dadi Janke was between us like a divine force pushing us together. I will never forget our mornings sitting on the roof with the morning prayers from the mosque surrounding us with their resonant call to God, while we had a lovely breakfast of a soft-boiled egg in a delicately patterned turquoise ceramic egg cup, two blocks of feta cheese, three Greek olives, and fresh bread and butter. Many of our dearest friends were there, including Gail and Franko Richmond who were working with the street kids teaching them our favorite song, The Time has Come. They also participated with us at a ceremony for peace and cooperation with the Secretary General and Barbara Pyle of CNN and also at the Peace Prayer Ceremony for the closing of the Wisdom Keepers.

Although I wasn't an official delegate for the Wisdom Keepers, I set up a series of interviews for Roger Watt with Rashmi Mayur, Noel Brown, Wangari Matthai, Millard Fuller, Kumar Ketkar, Dave Korten, Sister Jenna of Brahma Kumaris, and with the Sufi Master of the whirling dervishes, among others.

At the end of the conference, we had lots of material. I wrote a skeleton script for a short film and began editing. Dave and I went to the editing studio with Roger. We would start and end with the whirling dervishes, and Roger would do the voiceover. At the very end, Roger broke into a spontaneous poem, Morning Star. It the very same poem I had hanging above my bed in my apartment in DC. It was the perfect ending to our film, "Wisdom Keepers", chanted in rhythmic cadence to the backdrop of the dervishes. Later, we'd use the same poem at our wedding.

> *"Men of the Earth, brothers in eternity*
> *Shake your souls awake!*
> *The hour so long waited for, the Promised hour has come*
> *Over the dark firmament of suffering humanity,*
> *Is rising the Morning Star...."*

Dave and I had fun, and even checked out the local Hookah Bars, drank Turkish coffee and took a Turkish bath and soaked in the sights and sounds.

However, now that we had edited our movie and everyone was leaving, we only had a few more days. I had always wanted to go to Ephesus. Although I didn't grow up Catholic, I was fascinated with Mary and had wanted to visit the House of Virgin Mary since I was a little girl. Rumor has it that Saint John took her to this stone house after Jesus' resurrection to live for the rest of her earthly life. It is located in a tranquil area on Mount Koressos.

Oddly enough, although the place is constantly flooded with visitors, nobody was inside the simple cottage upon our arrival except for three nuns who were chanting. They turned around and the taller one said:

"Bless you for coming and we would like you to have these," as she put little gold medals with Mary's angelic face in our hands.

"You two are a very special couple," she said with a twinkle in her eye, and then all three of them turned around and walked out of the little cottage in unison.

We were alone in Mary's house, and we could see tourists milling around outside.

"We have been given this special time alone. Let's kneel at the altar and ask Divine Mother to fulfill our prayers to be of service to humanity," I suggested.

We knelt, and as I bowed my head, I could feel Dave staring at me. I glanced over and found him looking at me. Again, I could almost see sparkles around his head. He put his medal in my hand and took my medal in his hand as he tried to come up with the right words,

"I have been noticing how we complement each other, and we seem better together than we do apart…."

Oh no, he's gonna ask me to marry him! What should I do?

Dave didn't fit all my pictures. I had had six proposals before this, and each time, my inner voice shouted, No, No, No! But now, for the first time, my inner guiding voice was giving me the green light. As I listened intently, I could almost hear the words internally:

Say YES, and say yes NOW, or Destiny will change.

Shaking, I looked up and Dave did indeed ask me to marry him. He had not planned this and didn't even have a ring. Our medals would represent our commitment. Something pushed me from inside to jump off the cliff and through my fear. I gazed deep into his eyes and said, "Yes."

We were both in shock when we went outside, holding each other's hand tight, amidst the tourist crowd. I was scared— we both were — yet we started planning our lives together, including our wedding.

When we returned to the US, he gifted me a delicate golden ring with a diamond and a hummingbird on it. Later, when he came to visit me at my Mom's house in La Jolla, he surprised me with a brilliantly sparkling round, one-carat diamond engagement ring. Nobody else in this world knew me as well as Dave, not even my own mother.

Dave wanted us to have a private vows ceremony in the boundary waters of Minnesota in the vicinity of the Ojibwa tribe before our traditional wedding set for next April 27, 1997. It was a splendid Indian summer in late October of 1996 when the private ceremony was held, making me wonder if we had been married in a past life as well. Dave took this opportunity to introduce me to some of his dearest friends. Lynn Rogers, a very famous bear researcher, invited us to stay in his cabin. When we arrived, he was about 100 feet up in an old tree.

"Welcome, Comrades!" a huge voice boomed.

He gave us a ride around the lake and told us endearing stories about wild animals. But what stayed with me was my encounter with an 800-pound bear. That creature could have torn me to pieces, into a dinner feast. He gently licked salmon oil off my hand instead.

For our private vows ceremony, we ported (carried) a canoe from the road to the Boundary Waters and rowed for miles in search of *our island*. We finally reached a beautiful tiny piece of land, filled with tall white pine and oak trees that were just beginning to change their green color into vibrant hues of orange and red.

Trusting his intuition, Dave said, "This is it … is the island for our ceremony!"

It was already evening, and the full moon added to the magic of nature, our love, and our vows ceremony. Believe it or not, Dave and I had decided to include the Peace Pipe in it. If done with intention, smoking a Peace Pipe is a sacred pact between you and the Creator and whoever you smoke with. After we pitched our tent, we started a bonfire and rolled out a beautiful American Indian carpet. Then we stripped naked and sat in front of each other. Our skin glowed in the dark from the blazing flames as if enveloped by the bright light of our blissful souls. As Dave unwrapped the Pipe from the fox fur it was stored in, it shimmered with radiant power. Dave handmade it in 1970, when he returned from Vietnam, with his Ojibwa brothers from the medicine lodge as a symbol of making peace with the Great Spirit. He quarried stone from pipestone Minnesota, and carved the pipe carefully out of white pine. He never smoked it previous to that night.

My husband – what a delightful and sacred word – filled the pipe with knick-knick (sacred tobacco), and we inhaled it together. As the smoke filled our lungs, a high vibration enlivened our bodies, minds and spirits. Our hearts were bursting with joy and gratitude. We had probably made the best decision of our lives, a decision that would shape millions of lives.

Dave left his beautiful ranch in Half Moon Bay and moved in with me in Washington immediately after the wedding. We loved to entertain and had fun cooking together and adjusted to each other's presence without a glitch. It's not easy to suddenly have another person—even one you love dearly—in your private space when you're used to living alone, but we were so committed to one another and our relationship that we never let our old habits interfere with our bliss. In fact, we were so in love — still are — that we couldn't stand being one minute apart.

I wanted Dave to experience a mission with me, so we organized a small mission to Haiti to provide gifts to 100 orphans. A friend from the UN, Deborah Moldow, offered to join us and also donate a Peace Pole to plant at the orphanage. Thus, the children could participate in a peace pole ceremony and call upon the energies of peace and harmony for Haiti. I was grateful for both.

We gathered a group of about ten people and had them collect at least ten toys each. By the time we landed in Haiti, we had over 500 gifts and spent an entire night wrapping them (I had brought lots of wrapping paper, tape and scissors and ribbon). Everybody was amazed at all the great toys we had manifested, as we kept busy wrapping while laughing and joking.

The next day, we bussed the children from the orphanage to the auditorium that Catholic Relief Services (where we were staying) had helped arrange. I put on my Santa's helper outfit—-a short tunic in bright red with three inches of white trim, a big black belt around my waist, a Santa hat, and a jingle bell necklace. Most of us had Santa hats and were wearing red, and everybody was beaming with joy. From behind the curtain, I peered into the brightly lit room as our young guests, about 100, took their seats; I wished I could hug them all. Giggles and exclamations of excitement filled the warm air. The short trip away from the orphanage and being inside such an elegant place for the first time was already a big gift.

"Wait till they see their real gifts," I told Dave, who had volunteered to be Santa.

He hugged me and gave me a quick kiss on my forehead.

"Thank you for bringing me with you. I knew your mission was important, but now I understand why... My mission is your mission!"

My eyes welled up, and I would have said a lot if it wasn't already time for the children to meet Santa and receive their gifts. We soon noticed that none of the kids were opening their presents. At first we didn't understand—- but then realized they had never before received a wrapped gift. So Dave helped a little boy by showing him how to tear off the paper to find his gift. The other kids caught on right away and had so much fun making a big mess of the auditorium with paper everywhere.

Afterwards, Dave and I ventured outside and saw another 100 kids looking in through the bars of the fence. One little girl put her hand out as if asking for something, and I took off my jingle bell to give her. However, after that, I had nothing else to give.

I looked at the group of about 20 kids who had followed us outside and asked them,

"Do any of you have a present you can share with these kids who have none?"

Then, the most moving thing happened. A tiny boy named Little Jacques walked over and gave away one of his five toys, and then the other kids followed. These children had nothing, yet they were giving away the first gifts they were given. Nearly all the other children did the same and it seemed they were filled with joy as we made a game of cleaning up the auditorium.

That night, as we were reminiscing about our experience in the lobby of the Catholic Relief Services compound, I noticed another group of travelers—-two men and an older, but very gentle and elegant older woman. Still on a high from the day, I went over to them to introduce myself and share the amazing story of the orphans sharing their presents.

"The Haitians are, indeed, special. My name is Madame Mellon," the elegant lady said. "My husband and I started the Albert Schweitzer Hospital in the Artibonite Valley. These are two of the cleft palate doctors that work there. I'm going there tomorrow, and you are welcome to join me."

The rest of our group had to go back home, but Dave and I decided to join her for the adventure. Madame Mellon was extremely wealthy (she belonged to the Carnegie-Mellon family) but it was clear she had a social conscience, and both Dave and I loved her energy. I also loved how Dave was always up for adventure.

The next morning, we said goodbye to our team and met Madame Gwen Mellon in the lobby. We piled into her car for a three-hour drive, stopping only to buy a few coconuts. On the way, she explained how she and her late husband, Larimer, had established the hospital on the advice of their good friend, Albert Schweitzer. In 1952, Schweitzer was awarded the Nobel Peace Prize for his philosophy of "reverence for life and tireless humanitarian work."

She also explained that voodoo was still prevalent in the country-side, and because many people believed in it, it did work. Case in point: a very healthy friend of hers had refused to pay a man for fixing her sink, as the sink still didn't work properly, but it had made the man angry. Shortly after, the woman had found a voodoo doll on her doorstep with pins stuck in it, and she dropped dead the next day.

We drove through the villages with tiny houses painted in rainbow colors. As the sun began to set, the lack of streetlights coupled with multicolored Tupperware bowls resting on front porches turned the landscape into one of vibrant pastel lights. I was falling in love with this country, not knowing that, one day, we would live there.

Dave and I officially got married on April 27, 1997, in Washington, DC. People complain about how stressful weddings are, but ours wasn't. I was so happy to be with all my friends and family—a total of 150 special family and friends—-and have the ceremony in a church I loved. The building looked like an old gothic cathedral, but small and charming. It was made of stone and had an oval shaped red door similar to those built in the 14th century. Plus, it was a Swedenborg church.

Its founder, Emanuel Swedenborg, was a famous Swedish theologian, scientist, philosopher, and mystic. He believed that all of heaven is in a human form and being useful to others is the cornerstone to spiritual growth. We joined the church not only because we resonated with his ideas, but also because it allowed us to have our wedding ceremony there. In fact, the minister and members of the church were delighted with this idea and offered more support than we expected or wished for.

Arthur, a homeless gentleman in his forties, offered to sing. I suspected he lived in the church belfry. He loved Sundays when the church offered sandwiches and it seemed he would stock up for the week.

Dave and I graciously accepted his offer although we weren't sure what to expect. We were so busy with preparations that soon enough, we forgot about him.

The day of the wedding finally arrived. When the doors opened and I saw the church, it took my breath away. It was like a scene from the higher realms. I also forgot completely about being upset with how my hair had turned out. Dave was standing proudly near the altar and everything seemed lit with an astral glow. This was destiny!

Because my Dad was not alive, I asked my uncle David to walk me down the aisle. He was married to my Dad's sister, Mary Alice. They were my favorite relatives. Both of them shone with an inner light and I loved them very much.

Uncle David worked for the State Department and had been in the Ambassador position in Taiwan before he retired. Tall and elegant, he spoke with a slight English accent. Aunt Mary Alice was more like me. She was artistic, loving, and spiritual. She had adopted a guru in her travels, and as a diplomat's wife, she loved hosting parties for interesting people.

Trembling, I clutched the arm of my beloved uncle David, and we began to walk slowly down the aisle. Seeing so many loved ones calmed down the fast beating of my heart and put a big and blissful smile on my face. My dear friend, Sasha, from Campaign for the Earth, read my favorite poem, Morningstar, which we used as the backdrop to our Wisdom Keepers film.

I had forgotten about Arthur, but just before the marriage ceremony ended, a booming alto voice filled the church. There he was, his burly 190-lb frame standing in the church belfry with a scarf wrapped around his neck as if he had time-traveled from the Middle Ages, vocalizing the power and love of the universe into his voice as he was singing acapella "Amazing Grace." It seemed the great sound filled the room with holiness.

Then Dave and I lit our individual candles and blended them into one. On our knees, we took communion with a solemn vow to dedicate this union to birthing the Divine. As we did so, incense filled the air, adding to the otherworldly ambience. Happiness filled our hearts.

The reception took place right up the street at the Mexican Cultural Center, which the Mexican Ambassador offered to us as a sign of appreciation for helping Mexico with medical supplies. It was a grand structure with a huge, rich mahogany staircase leading to the upper floor, surrounded by artsy paintings. As Dave and I arrived, most of the guests were there, and I remember the MC announcing the arrival of the new Mr. and Mrs. Rivard.

We first had cocktails in the Gold Room, then had our first dance. Gail and Franko, our good friends, and many of the children there sang Franko's song, The Time Has Come. Later, we gifted our guests their CD, with the cover art of beautiful watercolor flowers that Gail had painted herself.

Next, the whole ballroom opened up as our dear friend, Sharon Franquemont (who had coordinated the Prayer Vigil on the Mall), sang the Lord's prayer acapella to bless our food. As guests ate, Sasha White, my roommate from Boulder and founder of the Campaign for the Earth, offered us a sacred dance. More gifts and surprises followed.

When the cake came out, Gail and Franko gifted us with champagne glasses with beautiful blue dolphins, commemorating our swim with the dolphins on the full moon when I first realized Dave was the right mate for me.

I was 44, the exact age a psychic guide had predicted I would marry my partner. At 30 years old, during a layover in Hawaii, she had told me I had to wait another 14 years before I would stand at the altar. She also said she was happy for me because it was no ordinary marriage. I would marry a partner who would support me in my mission of helping children and make a huge difference, she had said. She had been right.

CHAPTER 10
BABY?

Wedding day

I SHARED WITH Dave on our honeymoon night about the psychic's prediction; I also had another thing to share with him before we embarked on our trip to Bali, where we were celebrating our honeymoon. My period was a little late, but I thought that it was due to pre-wedding jitters. He burst into a huge smile.

"Well, we have to find out," he exclaimed, as called his brother Tony, whom we had planned to meet during our two-hour layover in Hawaii, on the way to Bali, asking him to pick up a pregnancy test and bring it to the airport.

Tony did meet us in Honolulu, a big, burly guy with flaming long red hair, the spitting image of a Viking. He gave me a huge bear hug, and I liked him instantly. We grabbed a cup of coffee in the lounge sharing all about the wedding. As we left, he handed us the package from the pharmacy.

"Good luck!" he said with a twinkle in his eye.

We departed for another 14-hour flight from Honolulu through Guam to Bali and we checked into the wedding suite in the gorgeous Intercontinental Bali Resort. I was so exhausted from the long trip that I didn't get up the nerve to try the pregnancy test until the next morning. The two blue lines showed I was with a child. My heart skipped a beat.

"Honey, we're pregnant! We're pregnant!" I exclaimed from the bathroom, already feeling the new life growing inside my body.

I expected a burst of enthusiasm, but silence followed, making me wonder if Dave was still in the other room.

"Honey, is everything ok?" I asked as I hurried out of the bathroom.

Dave was standing in front of the window, his eyes filled with tears. For once, this amazing man, who always spoke the right words at the right time, was speechless. The moment he saw me, he opened his arms, and I sheltered at his chest. When I looked up at him, his eyes were shining with infinite love and bliss. He must have seen the same in mine, for he gave me a passionate kiss before he spoke.

"I love you so much and I'm so happy. Thank you!"

"I love you …"

Our bodies and minds buzzed with excitement. We didn't really care if the baby was a boy or a girl. All that mattered was that we would have the flesh of our flesh to love and nurture.

Exhilarated with the thought of becoming parents, we toured the lush countryside, visited temples where we received a blessing from the monks, shared ceremonies with the locals in the temples, and ended up in the artsy town of Ubud. Our stay was like something out of a dream. By day, we got around on bicycles, passing by spirit houses. At night, we shared wonderful restaurants under twinkling lanterns, watched Ramayana dances, and languished in our love to the hypnotic sound of Balinese gamelan music, which filled the air spiced with cinnamon, jasmine, and honey.

Dave had always wanted to go to the famous island of Lombok and, just like him, I was always up for adventure. He suggested we ride a motorcycle to our destination—-I think he was still trying to impress me—and I agreed, not realizing that although Dave was an expert cyclist, motorcycles were a different entity altogether.

We drove the length of the island along a precarious cliff on the vehicle we rented from a local. Dave wasn't an expert at shifting, so several times we almost lost control. There was no barrier, and it was extremely dangerous. I uttered Hail Mary's, although I am not Catholic, while Dave did his best to keep us safe. He was determined to master that motorcycle and, like every time he sets a goal, he finally did.

We stopped at a quaint little hotel to rest and later in the afternoon, we rode to the shore for the sunset. We found a majestic beach with soft, white sand and bathed by huge waves, perhaps six to eight feet high. I just had to jump into the water, and Dave was right behind me. Never, even in Hawaii, had I felt the power of the roaring surf that strong. The great ocean immediately picked us up and tossed us as if we were tiny pieces of driftwood. Each wave plunged us violently downward to the ocean floor as sand entered every orifice in our bodies. We were lucky to stay in one piece and make it back to the shore, for if anything would have happened, there was no one around for miles.

The next day, Dave proudly announced he had a surprise for me. I immediately pictured a champagne brunch or couple massage at a lovely hotel, but needless to say, I was puzzled when Dave turned the bike onto some kind of field. His idea of a good time was snake hunting.

"So much for my dreams of a lovely meal," I muttered. The ground looked like a huge piece of Swiss cheese, filled with holes, only brown. A few minutes later, Dave yelled as if somebody stabbed him in the heart.

"What's wrong?" I asked, but before he could even answer, it was my turn to scream as I felt a searing pain as if someone had shot me in the arm. Those holes were actually wasp nests—-huge hornet wasps—-the kind that kill water buffalos.

What followed resembles a scene in a comedy movie, and I would have laughed if we weren't the protagonists. Dave pulled the bike out of the field and to a stop. When he hopped off the bike to look at me, a huge wasp was hovering next to my head, ready for another strike. Desperate situations require desperate measures so Dave started beating me over my head to save me from the sting. Back at the hotel, we laid next to each other in bed under mosquito netting for two days, moaning in agonizing pain. Not your typical honeymoon.

About a month after we returned from our honeymoon to Washington, DC, we went to the Vietnam Veterans Memorial. Dave had lost a friend in the war named Carl Culp. Imagine two acres of monuments dedicated to the service members of the U.S. Armed Forces who died in South East Asia and those who were unaccounted for during the war. It was eerie to be in a place commemorating death as a new life was growing inside my womb. I was a few weeks into my new pregnancy, surrounded by a cocoon of love and magic, feeling more inspired and alive than ever. Only a woman that has carried a child, even for a short time, can experience this amazing creative power and the unique fulfillment it brings. Two hearts literally beating inside her body, two souls merging together, a blessed wholeness.

As I was walking around the monument, mumbling Dave's friend's name and gazing at thousands of the names engraved on the black shiny marble, hoping to find a match, one of the Park Rangers, a slender woman with cerulean blue eyes, followed me.

"Are you saying Carl Culp?" she asked.

"Yes, we're looking for his name on the monument. He was a friend of my husband who served with him in Vietnam."

"Are you kidding me? I've been looking for you, guys for years. My name is Suzanne Sigona," she said as she reached out to shake both of our hands. "Force Recon was one of the most celebrated and famous units in Vietnam! I have contact with most of your team!"

I interrupted her stories when I felt a sharp pain in my womb and said to Dave we needed to get home. He helped me walk the six blocks to our apartment while I endured horrible cramps, doubling me over in pain. We had lovingly named the baby "Egbert". It was terrifying to think I might lose him. Maybe the wasp bite on the island of Lomback was to blame? Dave felt helpless and offered to drive me to the hospital, but I realized it was too late. It was our second miscarriage. I carried this precious soul for only 12 weeks, yet the pain of losing him was unbearable. For days, I felt empty inside and blamed myself for not listening to my intuition and acting reckless during our honeymoon in Bali. Eventually, I found solace in helping more children in a different way. They weren't biologically mine, but because we are all connected as one, they were part of me.

Soon afterwards, I met a flight attendant who volunteered to escort children in need of medical care to the United States. She explained that the program was run by former Eastern Airlines Passenger Service Agent, Margaret Whitehead. This was a unique way that flight attendants could bring love into action and I knew I had to meet her. I flew to Peachtree City, Georgia to meet Margaret and her husband and asked if she would like to run Airline Ambassadors. American Airlines had a program to provide flights for the children—-AA Miles for Kids in Need. She politely declined but offered to run our Children's Medical Escort Program. I said yes, and soon after, she arranged our first trip.

American Airlines flight attendant Rachel Martinez, based in Miami, escorted our very first child, Maria Jose. Everything ran like clockwork. However, American Airlines was unfamiliar with this program, and sometimes things did not go as planned, as you'll find out by reading Leeanne Hansen's story.

Leeanne Hansen (Leela) was a drop-dead gorgeous blond and a flight attendant for AA based in LA. She had heard about AAI and signed up as a member as well as a volunteer for the Children's Medical Escort Program. She was excited to escort for the first time a child traveling to receive medical care. Her assignment was to escort four-year-old Katerina Mendez back to Honduras as her surgery was complete in Boston and it was time for her to return to her family. Leela picked up Katerina in Boston from a Healing the Children Representative and flew with her to Miami. The child was on a Miles for Kids in Need full-fare ticket and Leela was using her airline passes. Waiting at the gate in Miami, Katerina was issued a ticket for 12A, and was sitting on Leela's lap, waiting until the very last minute when standby tickets were given out. When the agent called Leeanne Hansen, she jumped up to grab her ticket.

"I'm sorry, Ms. Hansen, you didn't make it. We will book you on the next flight," the agent said. Leela's face turned red and she started to shake.

"You are not separating me from Katerina! I'm bringing her home to Honduras after medical care. I *am* her legal guardian and I will not leave her. If I am not going, then she's not going!"

There was no convincing the agent.

"I'll be glad to book you both on the flight tomorrow morning. However, you are on a standby ticket, so we can't be sure, but your chances of making it tomorrow look much better."

Leela put in a call to Margaret Whitehead, who calmly told her she did the right thing and to simply get a hotel room at the airport Hotel MIA. She would be reimbursed for her expenses, as well as providing dinner for the girl at an airport restaurant. Leela was still shaking when she entered the MIA Hotel room.

"We have to pray," she exclaimed, as she dropped her bag.

Both Leela and Katerina got on their knees beside the bed with their hands together in prayer position. Leela started asking God for strength and then she began to cry and sob, her head shaking. Then she felt Katerina's hand patting her back and took it as an answer from God's littlest angel. The next day, both had seats on the plane.

There were other amazing stories of escorts during the early days, like Masako Doi, who brought a little boy all the way from New York to Burkina Faso. She had been up for 24 hours and all she wanted to do was sleep. However, the village had a different idea. They hosted a wild welcome party with a fire and African dancing and drumming that went well into the night. They even gave her a few glasses of bissap/bisap, a special drink made from hibiscus flowers. She finally fell into bed in the small hut, exhausted, only to awake a few hours later to pee. There was no bathroom in the hut, only a small outhouse outside. As she ventured to the location, she heard a loud squawk, and a huge parrot, about a foot high, landed on her head. It wasn't funny then, but now she laughs about being attacked by a parrot in Burkina Faso.

Then there was the story of Alexander Wahl, who escorted little Lovelie Jean back from heart surgery to her home in Mirebelais, Haiti. There were no phones in those days in remote Haiti and Lovelie had been gone for eight months. The community and her family thought she had died. When Alexander, in his flight attendant uniform, came walking her up the road of the village, the women let out the typical Haitian screams.

"Li vivian! Li vivian, Lovelie li vivian!"----meaning, "(She lives, she lives, Lovelie lives").

Believing the little girl had risen from the dead, they gathered palm fronds to welcome them and celebrate her joyous reunion with her family.

Then there was the baby Maddox Chivan from Cambodia, who was adopted in 2002 by Angelina Jolie, facilitated by AAI member Lauryn Galindo. Reflecting on this in 2020, Jolie explained, "Cambodia was the country that made me aware of refugees. It made me engage in foreign affairs in a way I never had and join UNHCR. Above all, it made me a mom."

Two months after our honeymoon, Dave was offered a job in San Francisco and we decided to move back to California from DC. We rented a small apartment in the darling town of Burlingame, within walking distance from Starbucks and libraries and I put in my transfer with AA to fly out of SFO. As a newlywed couple, our life was an endless joy.

Well, life wasn't always all roses. First, there were the reptiles ...

Soon after we moved into our new apartment, I had visions of decorating it beautifully as a welcoming and uplifting ambience to all who crossed our threshold. So when Dave suggested adding a menagerie of snake cages in the living room, I totally freaked out and ran to Elisabet Sathouris' condo, just down the street.

"What in the world have I done, Elisabet?" I asked. "Dave doesn't get me! I won't live with a living room full of reptile cages!"

"Calm down, Nancy!" Elisabet said. "Dave is first an environmentalist—-snakes can look elegant in cages with plants and the proper lighting."

At that point, I began to sob. Ambience had always meant so much to me and creating beauty and an uplifting environment was a part of my soul. If Dave went through with his project, I could not be happy. When I got up the courage to tell him how I felt, he wrapped his arms around me.

"Honey, you are the woman and can be in charge of the house. What you say will go," he said.

We kissed and hugged and made passionate love that night.

Dave's office was within walking distance from our apartment, and I had joined the gym nearby his office. After my workouts, I would stick my head inside his office to say hi. He would sneak home whenever he could to make love to me because we were trying to make another baby. He was still my best friend, supporting me in my mission to bring love into action, encouraging, and comforting me when I was sad. He always lifted the heaviness weighing on my shoulders just by wrapping his arms around me. My heart wasn't that into being a flight attendant anymore, especially since they had turned down again my request to support my humanitarian work. I needed a break from flying—-I was considering a leave of about six months—-and Dave backed my decision. Knowing the Mayor of San Francisco, he was also able to help me get an office for Airline Ambassadors at the prestigious World Trade Center on the wharf of San Francisco Bay! I was so excited—-our first real Airline Ambassadors office!

A few months into our new life in Burlingame, AAI became overwhelming because we started putting out an eight-page monthly newsletter. I made friends with the people at Colorprint and they helped with design. Friends came over to our house to help. Our tiny apartment was often crammed with 20-30 people, as I'd hold meetings there. We were getting so many donations we needed a warehouse. Stanford Hospital was a regular donor—they gave us thousands of dollars' worth of products. Then there was the robbery.

Last, but not least, there was another pregnancy. At some point, in this crazy yet beautiful life, I realized I may be pregnant again, as Dave and I were trying hard. I also had a profound dream where Sai Baba, the Indian Guru I visited after Daddy died, appeared in a shining light.

"*I came to check on you and Dave, do you have any questions? I also came to warn you there are people working against you,*" he said.

I didn't believe that people were working against me; I was so naïve and oblivious to the gossip running around, but I did want to know one thing.

"*Baby?*" I asked.

Sai Baba looked at me so deeply and lovingly—I felt I would fall into his fathomless eyes.

"*No baby! Your work is with the world's children.*"

I knew then that I would have a miscarriage, and soon afterwards I did. Deep inside I knew Sai Baba was right. In a way, all the children of the world, especially those whom we escorted or needed health care or finding a loving family, were my children. And Dave had the Earth, its environment, and animals that needed to be nurtured and protected with the same love a father would have raising his son.

I didn't bring a baby into the world, but fell in love with Yorkshire terriers and became the mother of one. Within a month after my third miscarriage, our little Yorkie, Lulu, came into our lives. We loved her dearly and she taught us how unconditional love can be expressed in so many different ways to everything and everybody around us.

CHAPTER 11
AAI POSTCARDS
FROM '98-'99

In Macedonia, with kids from Kosovo

IN AUGUST 1998, Airline Ambassadors International mobilized 6,000 pounds of medical supplies and clothing to help the Legion of Goodwill's charitable work in Brazil. I kissed Dave goodbye—-he was busy with jobs with the Asian Arts Center and the Bart Airport extension in San Francisco—-and had to stay home.

The bright lights of TV cameras met us upon arrival, and, by the end of the week, we felt like celebrities. Our group visited day care centers, schools and old folks homes in Rio de Janeiro and São Paulo. We joined the members of the Legion in some of the worst favelas (slums), helping them to bring warm, wholesome food to the families. One evening, we looked out of our hotel in downtown Rio and noticed a dozen Legion volunteers on the street corner. They were feeding the homeless delicious organic food and also had set up a medical table to wash the feet and wounds of street people, shave them, and give them haircuts. The volunteers radiated an inner light and happiness I had rarely seen. I began to cry; never in my life had I seen such selfless sharing and sincere joy. I had to join them.

"What did you think about your visit?" I asked 18-year-old Gibran. He had joined the trip as one of our youth volunteers and I thought he might complain about the long bus ride that day.

He slowly raised his head and looked at me, his dark eyes glistening.

"This trip has been the pivotal experience of my lifetime," he replied.

It felt so wonderful; sharing this vision was having the impact I had hoped for!

Hurricane Mitch was one of the most powerful and deadly tropical cyclones seen in the modern era. Mitch passed through Central America from October 22 to November 5 and caused billions of dollars in material losses. On October 25, I received a letter from a minister and his wife in Honduras asking for help.

"Nobody knows the tragedy of the situation in Honduras. The streets are full of dirty water, garbage and desperate people. Many haven't eaten for four days. People have been stranded on rooftops for the past couple of nights with no food or water. The mosquitos and flies have begun to multiply and, as soon as the water goes down, hundreds of dead bodies and animals will contaminate everything. Help us please, anything you can do will help," he wrote.

I called a meeting of our core team to see what we could do. Leanne Hansen—Leela, the same woman who had escorted Katarina back to her village in Honduras—said she would do a drive for donations at LAX and requested a drop off point at LAX Cargo. Kenneth Key of Missions Unlimited in Jasper, Alabama, who had worked in Honduras before, wanted to provide 100 "Love Buckets" - huge plastic buckets full of emergency supplies. At that time, we were still sharing buddy passes and I offered him one if he would help arrange the itinerary for Honduras. The team would also visit Nicaragua that also sustained damage.

Leeane had no idea how generous the Honduran community in Los Angeles could be when she asked them to drop off aid at the American Airlines terminal. Five semi-trucks drove up with 150,000 lbs of food, water, medicine and clothes, plenty to fill a 747 freighter!

I received a call from American Airlines LAX Cargo on Saturday morning, November 7th, as I was having my morning coffee.

"Are you Nancy, President of Airline Ambassadors?"

"Yes, that's me."

"You have 181 pallet loads of cargo in our warehouse from Airline Ambassadors' drive for Honduras. It's taking up all the space, and it's interfering with airline operations. You have 24 hours to get it out."

"I'll be there this afternoon," I said, already planning in my mind my flight to Los Angeles.

I had no idea how we were going to do this, but immediately called Leela to meet me at the airport. I inwardly called to God and the Angels for help. Amazingly, once again, my prayer was answered.

Leela contacted J.B. Hunt Trucking to move the aid and Green Valley warehouse to keep it there while we sorted the cargo. She put out the word to the Honduran community that we needed volunteers to sort the aid and also to raise $70,000 within a week to pay Operation USA to move the cargo by private plane. As impossible as it seemed, we did it!

The plan was for us to meet the plane and Operation USA team with an Airline Ambassadors banner on November 14th to do a photo shoot for Fox News, who agreed to meet us there and cover our mission to Honduras. Our team would leave the next day. I planned to stay at Leela's house that night since Dave was working too many jobs in San Francisco to join us on this one.

Before I continue this story, I need to insert a little family background.

Dave and I had planned to fly to meet my Mom and sister in Las Vegas for an early Thanksgiving to visit old family friends, Will and Sue Crenshaw, and their daughter Melissa. I told Mom we had received 181 pallets of aid at LAX Airport and raised $70,000 for the flight to Honduras for victims of Hurricane Mitch.

"Please don't talk about that. I'm not interested," my Mom said harshly. "Do not even mention Airline Ambassadors when you are with the Crenshaws. They don't care about it. You have to promise me!"

Dave and I planned to meet Mom and Cheryl in Las Vegas, but we missed the first flight out of San Francisco and Mother was furious. It was Friday the 13th and, although I'm not superstitious, I thought it had something to do with it.

We made the second flight and arrived at the time they were having dinner. Dave had a great idea.

"Honey, let's give them a good laugh. We know they are having dinner at the restaurant Noodles in the Bellagio. Their reservation is for the early bird special at 5 p.m. Our flight now arrives at 5 p.m., so let's just go right over. We will arrange with the waiter to pay for their dinner so they will get a pleasant surprise and you and I can don a disguise. We'll be waiting for them near the slot machines as they finish. It will be hilarious and your Mom won't stay mad."

When we made it to the Bellagio, I bought a blond wig and sunglasses and Dave got a Panama hat, a fake mustache and a cigar. We snuck over to Noodles restaurant and saw in the back Mom, Cheryl, and Cheryl's nine-year-old son, Travis. Dave gave the cashier our credit card and instructions to tell the family that their dinner had been paid for by someone anonymous.

We positioned ourselves at the slot machines so they would walk by us as they left. Mom and Cheryl walked right by, but young Travis wasn't fooled a bit— he had been ring bearer at our wedding and didn't miss a trick. He stopped right in front of me.

"Nancy, when did you color your hair?"

Mom was still furious that we had missed our flight, so our plan didn't exactly work.

The following day, we met at Melissa's house at 11 a.m. for an early Thanksgiving dinner. Melissa didn't have a long enough tables for eight people so she had set up two card tables with festive tablecloths and decorations.

One for Melissa and Sue, her mom, me and Dave, and one for Cheryl, Travis, my Mom, and Will Crenshaw. We had a lovely dinner, but it was during the pumpkin pie that Mrs. Crenshaw learned that Dave and I had to catch a flight to Los Angeles that night at 5 p.m.

"Why do you have to go tonight?" she asked.

I tried to speak softly so Mom wouldn't hear, and explained we were meeting the Fox News team to see off the airplane of aid for survivors of Hurricane Mitch, and I was leaving on a week-long mission to Honduras and Nicaragua the next day.

"Nancy," my Mom shrieked in a disapproving tone from the next table,

"Remember what you and I talked about?"

"Well, Mom, Mrs. Crenshaw asked me a direct question and I did not want to lie."

After that outburst, the whole atmosphere was so tense that Dave and I were greatly relieved to leave and be on our way to the airport again.

When we got to the Operation USA plane on the LAX tarmac, we draped the Airline Ambassadors banner over the aid for a quick photo shoot. Fox TV met us the following morning and covered the takeoff. Some reporters traveled with us to Honduras. At last, we were off.

Ken Key had arranged a school bus to transport our aid and to visit a medical clinic, housing projects, and refugee camps. We made the huge mistake of passing out Beanie Babies and other toys to the kids from the bus and nearly caused a riot.

In Nicaragua, we ventured by horseback high into the mountains to the remote community of Bocay, which one of our teams had visited before. An older woman in a blue kerchief invited us to visit her house. In the center of the living room wall were her prized possessions, a 3x4-inch family portrait from a Kodak instamatic camera, a Beanie Baby, and the Airline Ambassadors round sticker that said "May Peace Prevail on Earth." It made me so happy to realize our work was affecting lives.

The weather was so hot that I jumped into a river, not realizing that the river could contain waterborne pathogens. I was sick as a dog leaving Bocay, lying in the back of the pickup truck on the drive out in agony, wearing one of those light blue medical masks. I couldn't wait to be in Dave's arms.

Unexpected but great news greeted me upon my arrival. The Vice President of Flight Service at American Airlines had approved a grant for $5,000 to support excess baggage for our teams to deliver humanitarian aid and tickets for the child escorts. This was our first corporate grant, and I felt that things were finally turning around.

Missions were now leaving nearly every month. In 1998 we had missions to Ecuador, Guatemala, Brazil, Bosnia, Dominican Republic, Haiti, Honduras, and Nicaragua. We had come a long way since we had started.

In the spring of 1999, AAI presented a panel on Sustainable Tourism at the United Nations. Chris Clousner, the VP of Northwest Airlines, participated from the corporate side along with luminaries such as: Dr. Noel Brown, former Director of the UN Environment Program; Dr. Rashmi Mayur of the International Institute for Sustainable Tourism; Lou D'Amore, President of the International Institute of Peace through Tourism; and Scott Wayne of the World Travel and Tourism Council. Twenty-six Airline Ambassador representatives from different airlines attended and were interviewed on tourism and volunteerism. Nane Annan, the UN Secretary General's wife, met with our team and this connection proved useful for our efforts in Macedonia.

I contacted her soon after and told her we wanted to help in response to the Kosovo crisis and asked if she could arrange an introduction to the United Nations High Commission on Refugees (UNHCR) so we could bring a team of humanitarians to the refugee camps.

She could not have been more supportive and thus 32 of us flew to Macedonia in June 1999. Our group included the famous Dr. Patch Adams and a team of 15 clown doctors. Little did we know what we were in for.

The feature film "Patch Adams" came out in 1998 about the life of Hunter Adams, and his belief that laughter is the best medicine. He founded Gesundheit Institute, which besides providing free health care, provides training for clown doctors.

Soon after arriving in Macedonia, we were met by UNHCR and driven first to Camp Cegrane. At the checkpoint, Dave noticed the big shiny barrel of a huge cannon (55 mm Howitzer) aimed down at us with soldiers milling around it polishing the barrel. We had assumed NATO provided protection, as First Lady Clinton and Senator Biden had visited the camp a day earlier.

The Camp director, a big brawny Albanian, and Dave started talking. Dave asked him about the Howitzer, as it seemed to be on the Serbian side of the mountain.

"Do not look up there and just pretend you do not notice," he replied.

"Why doesn't the NATO Commander just order the phantom jets flying around the Camp to take out the Howitzer?" Dave whispered in my ear far enough from the Camp director. The same question sat on the tip of my tongue, and, to this day, we never got a clear answer.

Later in the afternoon, I asked about the fires that suddenly appeared in a seemingly peaceful valley below. The Albanian Camp director said the Serb troops were burning down the villages. They had been keeping the same schedule for weeks, on the same day, at around 5 p.m. Shortly after, hundreds of Kosavars stormed the border gate entry into the camp, desperately screaming and crying. It turned out the Serbs had gunned down a crowd of refugee families as they lined up to cross the border into Macedonia.

I'll never forget the tears in the eyes of one man who had been in line behind his wife and seen her shot down in front of him. I felt so terribly helpless.

The refugees told us how they were forced from their homes at gunpoint and had to hide for weeks or months in the forests. They had witnessed the brutal death of women and children and watched their homes and villages burn.

Previously, many of them had good middle-class lives and owned a business. They were also friends with their Serbian neighbors. But when the war began, neighbor turned against neighbor. Christian Serbs turned against the Muslim Kosovars, much like what happened in WW2 when Hitler turned the Christians against the Jews. It was unbelievable to me that humanity was still capable of this, but here it was in front of me. At the time of the publication of this book, it looks like history is repeating itself. Therefore, I would like to remind you that, at a deep level, we are all one. Division is a form of control and it can never happen without our consent. We always have a choice: to love or to hate one another. At this point in time, all we need is love.

While bombs rattled the ground, we walked through rows of tents, visited with refugees, and gave toys to children. They loved the gifts, but loved even more knowing that they weren't alone and forsaken and that somebody out there cared for them.

"Thank God you've come," one refugee woman exclaimed. "You have brought your love and you have helped our children laugh again."

The next day we met with the NATO General and officially handed out the large medical donation that we had brought. We introduced him to Patch and his clown doctors suggesting they could provide entertainment for the kids. Patch automatically attracts attention with his 6'4" frame and streak of purple down his long graying hair. The group didn't exactly fit in with the military feel, but all the clowns stood up, and the General smiled—-he was in.

Camp Cegrane was receiving 50,000 refugees a day, and roads needed to be kept clear for water and food trucks. The General insisted that none of us begin our activities until he got us to the designated area and he gave the green light. I should have realized there could have been a problem when Patch slipped a whoopee cushion under the General's seat just before he sat down.

"You heard the General. Tomorrow's trip is about getting the lay of the land first. Don't start clowning until he gives us the ok," I warned Patch as our host took a short break to answer an urgent call. Patch looked down at me, a mischievous twinkle in his eyes.

"Clowns break rules," he replied.

I should have known then there may be trouble, but decided not to push it and keep cordial relations going with the clown doctors—-so I bit my tongue.

At the end of the meeting, I told the General about the Children's Peace Quilt, a project initiated by Beverly Britton, my inspirational girlfriend. I wanted to involve 100 children from the camp in this project and ask them to express their vision of a peaceful world. We had brought paints, crayons, and Muslin fabric squares. These squares would be sewn into a Children's Peace Quilt.

The passion in my voice must have been contagious, for he arranged a tent for us.

Irene Logan, a DCA-based flight attendant, joined me in the tent, which was set up with little school desks just for us. The children were eager to participate, but we did not get pictures of peace, for their imagination reflected the horrors of the world; their drawings were bloody, with pregnant women being stabbed and rooster heads chopped off. I guess they needed to get their pain out before they could begin to heal (we later displayed the Peace Quilt they made at the Cannon Rotunda at the US Congress and at conferences around the world). Inspired by this letter-writing program to connect the young refugees to their counterparts in the United States, we also delivered letters from children in San Francisco and offered to return their responses. By the time I walked down the hill in Camp Cegrane, my arms full of muslin pieces and letters, everything seemed to work according to the plan. That was until I saw Dave frantically motioning to me to come quickly. My heart skipped a bit, afraid the Horowitz was about to fire at us.

The situation wasn't that bleak but still didn't look good. The clowns had not waited for the General to get them to a secure area and created a dangerous riot. They had done everything he had told them not to do, blocking the way for emergency vehicles carrying water and food and putting everyone in the camp in jeopardy. Dave had to fix their mess and get them onto the bus. But the worst part was that Airline Ambassadors was not welcome back.

The next challenge was to actually get the yellow school bus that had been carrying our team out of the camp. Picture hundreds of children gathered around it and you'll understand. Plus, the clowns weren't helping. They were sticking their heads out the windows and, led by Patch's loud and resonant voice, were singing a popular '60s song "Da Doo Ron Ron, Da Doo Ron Ron!". It seemed like 1,000 children chased us as we drove away.

Although my dad was an officer and a graduate of the Naval Academy, I never believed in the military and felt bad that I did not honor him with that respect when he was alive. But my trip to Macedonia helped me to see from a different perspective. I appreciated their dedication to protecting those they loved and their bravery in risking their lives for a higher purpose. After hearing so many stories of slaughter and violence in the former Yugoslavia, I was proud when the US sent in troops to stop the massacre. It's unbelievable and outrageous what men can inflict upon one another.

On our way home, Dave and I stopped in Ljubljana, which is paradise on Earth. I guess we needed to remember what life could be beyond the horror and terror of the war. Small black roads meandered through emerald green grass and patches of pine trees to small idyllic hamlets. We spent the night and sang with the locals at a small pub, our hearts filled with camaraderie, goodwill, and hope that humans can live in harmony, peace, and acceptance of one another. I was determined to do everything in my power to make that happen.

As if the Universe was giving me a nod, shortly after our mission in Macedonia, I got my first major award for my humanitarian work. The International Peace Prayer Day organization honored me as 1999 Woman of Peace and my great mentor, Millard Fuller, founder of Habitat for Humanity, as Man of Peace. Additionally, Golden Temple Natural Foods awarded Airline Ambassadors a Peace Cereal Grant of $5,000.

The ceremony took place in a lovely outside setting in Espanola, New Mexico to an audience of 2,000 with dozens of families and lots of children too. I noticed they had a different demeanor than those in Kosovo and Macedonia, as if the kids that had been broken by disaster had so much more gratitude and humility than the children from the United States who seemed much more selfish. Because of my award, AAI became a hot topic in the media.

By that time, we had already received coverage in dozens of feature articles. I kept all the clippings in a dedicated scrapbook and even framed an excellent article from the Dallas Morning News, "Hearts with Wings," about a mission to El Salvador. My fascination with that beautiful country must have first begun then.

CHAPTER 12
OUR FIRST WINGS

Unloading aid for Haiti

ALL THE AAI girls fell in love with Willam Dise, the American Airlines Denver Regional Director and Crew Chief. He was a gorgeous black guy, with a fabulous smile and a 6'3" frame, not to mention his open and kind heart. He was working hard to support AAI, and managed to charm Bob Baker, VP of Operations for

American Airlines, to approve a 757 Boeing airplane to be donated to Airline Ambassadors.

That donation included the pilots, crew, and fuel. William explained the plane would only be on the ground with time to unload and immediately get back into service. We had to make that short window work! The trip was scheduled to leave in one month from Denver to Haiti, and William already had 2,000 pounds of donated paint he was planning on bringing to an orphanage, recommended by the NGO—Food for the Poor.

William was hoping that Dave and I would be able to join him on the trip and help him fill the plane with humanitarian aid (30,000 pounds' available cargo space).

I promised him we would clear our schedules and help with the aid. However, after so many rejections from American Airlines, a part of me doubted the wonderful news I had just received.

There was only one way to find out: call Jane Allen, VP of American Airlines Flight Service. She confirmed everything William had said, adding that the volunteers could ride down on the plane but would have to use their airline passes to get back home.

The next call was to Rodney from LDS Charities, funded by the Mormon Church. It's the largest humanitarian organization in the world. I asked him what kind of humanitarian aid LDS Charities could provide for a trip to Haiti. He said they had school kits, hygiene kits, newborn kits and nonfat dry milk and would be glad to deliver the full 30,000 lbs. That's when I knew I had to put my scheduled trip on the trip trade board so another flight attendant could pick it up and free an entire week for me. Dave also took time off from his company, Steel Reinforcing Incorporated.

A month went by in a blink of an eye, and the day of our mission to Haiti arrived. As Dave and I made our way to the American Airlines gate at Denver International Airport, I heard a voice screaming my name.

"Is that Nancy Rivard?"

I looked over my shoulder, where it came from, and saw a sexy young woman with long blond hair. She was as shapely as a former Playboy Bunny but couldn't have weighed over 100 lbs. I knew that for sure, as within a couple of seconds, she jumped into my arms and wrapped both legs around me.

"Suzy! Suzy Kraybacher from Mercy and Sharing Foundation in Aspen!" I exclaimed.

Her husband, Joe, stood by smiling. I had called Suzy when William told me that they would be on the trip, and our team also planned to visit the Mercy and Sharing facility.

We continued to the gate together and met other friends of William, about 30 in total: ticket agents, flight attendants, and a few young people with their parents. Everyone was hyped. Then Crew Chief, William Dise, showed up to welcome everyone, his forehead covered in sweat. "I just finished loading every inch of that airplane with the humanitarian contribution from LDS Charities," he said, catching his breath.

Dave and I were in seat 12B and C and next to us was a carton of dried milk, a bag of school supplies, and a little crib. We settled in for our almost six-hour flight, hoping we could rest and make up for the difference in time zones. But the atmosphere on board was euphoric, so there was no way we could sleep. When we landed, there was some hold up, (as this was not a normal flight.) The pilots did not have much time to turn the plane around and we had to be quick in unloading all the aid. William and a few others hopped outside first to off-load the freight and the rest of us helped with the aid stuffed in the overhead bins, under and in the seats. We quickly learned the most efficient way to do this was to form a human chain, where one person passed to the other, and positioned ourselves from inside the plane, down the stairs to the tarmac, where we stacked everything neatly (we ended up adopting this technique for all of our missions). When we finally finished, we met with the Food for the Poor representatives to hand over our cargo. My intuition told me to keep a little crib in the van that was taking us around.

On our first day, at the Mercy and Sharing Abandoned Baby Unit, Haiti showed us her other face, unknown to the millions of tourists for whom it is one of the most beautiful tropical paradises. Upon entering the room, the pain and suffering of the abandoned children permeated my very soul. In almost every case, the children did not have names, birth certificates or a past that was known. Most of them, often left for dead on the hospital steps, were severely handicapped and the victims of neglect and abuse. Some were formerly "restaveks"- children in servitude to a master. Mercy and Sharing provided these children with food, clothing, clean water, medical visits, and loving care.

At the time of our trip, Haiti was home to 750,000 orphans, many of whom had living parents. Forced by poverty, parents were giving up their rights, hoping their children would receive food, shelter and education. I racked my brain to figure out what I would do if I were in their shoes? What would be more selfish: giving away my child and telling myself she would have a better life or keeping her, hoping for a twist of fate. Was there something to be done to help the families stay together? Although I couldn't come up with a satisfying answer, at least I knew I would do everything I could to make their lives a little brighter.

Our next visit started early in the morning, at the "House of Hope", a Catholic orphanage with about sixty children. Our goal was to paint the entire building. William and Dave stood out as expert painters as everybody on our team did their part. Halfway through the day, I took a short break from the heat to rest in the living room. My rest was interrupted when there was a knock on the door and one of the nuns answered it.

A young man dressed in shabby clothes stood outside holding a basket with a newborn baby covered in a tiny green blanket. With a pained expression on his face, he asked if the House of Hope would take the child. The nun declined; all beds were filled.

"Dear Sister, I actually have a crib in our van outside," I chirped, happy I had followed my gut.

"If it's God's Will and there is a crib, we will take this little lamb," the nun said. Her decision was part of my gratitude prayer that night. As I got into bed and cuddled in Dave's loving arms, my intuition kicked in again,

"Darling, we will be back," I told him. "And we'll stay longer."

I don't know if it was the blessings of Haiti for helping her children, but as soon as we got back home from our mission we rode a wave of good fortune. San Francisco Chronicle ran a feature story on Airline Ambassadors International, and San Francisco Magazine wrote a big article, and Autobiography Magazine did a spread on us as well as a photo shoot of me in front of a Boeing 767 at San Francisco International Airport. And then I got a call from the lovely Loretta Swit who played nurse Major Margaret Houlihan aka Hot Lips in the TV series *M.A.S.H.*

It was the first day in our new office in San Mateo when I heard her voice at the other end of the receiver. She had learned about us from an article in the *Biography Magazine* while perusing magazines in her dentist's office and wanted to help. I was looking for a celebrity spokesperson, and she was perfect.

"This is fabulous, Loretta. Thank you so much," I said. "How about being our Celebrity Spokesperson?"

"Are you kidding me, I'd love to," she replied, in her crystal-bell bubbly voice. Next we knew, we were planning our first meeting, a nice dinner at an Italian restaurant across the street from my office. Ken Behring, an American real estate developer, former owner of the Seattle Seahawks, founder of Wheelchair Foundation, and one of the largest donors in the world, joined us since he was a big fan of the actress and a strategic partner for Airline Ambassadors International. We saw a lot of possibilities of working together. Loretta agreed to join us on an upcoming mission to China.

Ken also asked if Airline Ambassadors would be willing to hand deliver wheelchairs and invited Dave and me to accompany him on his private plane to deliver wheelchairs to Africa. Of course we would. A huge opportunity presented itself; not only were we going to hang out and build a stronger connection with one of the richest men in the world, but also get a chance to find new opportunities to bring love into action in countries such as South Africa, Namibia, and Mozambique.

It was my first time as a flight attendant on a private jet. Ken's elegant airplane was top of the line and looked like a luxury condo, with its state-of-the-art amenities, dining rooms, and bedrooms. We stopped on the East Coast to pick up Randy Smoak, the President of the American Medical Association, and his wife; and then in Milan, for the famous designer, Stephano Ricci; and twelve bicyclists who would bike from Cape Town, South Africa, to Windhoek, Namibia to raise funds for the Wheelchair Foundation. As it turned out, Stephano was tailoring a special suit for Hosni Mubarak, the President of Egypt at the time, which led to my first visit to Egypt. The perk of being on a private jet is that you can stop whenever you want, wherever you want, as long as you have clearance. So we made a stop in Egypt for Stefano to work on his project. As soon as he returned, we continued to Karnak, where we spent the night and enjoyed a spectacular midnight tour of the Valley of the Kings in Karnak. Although we were in Egypt only 24 hours, it was magical.

The flight to Cape Town, South Africa, lasted ten hours. Part of me wished I joined the twelve bicyclists on their 918-mile trip to Namibia, but we had other adventures in store.

We met with Nelson Mandela and his wife, Graca Machel, at their home located on the outskirts of Cape Town. I remember trembling in the silk olive-green jacket I bought just for the trip, partly with excitement and partly with the cool breeze. What an honor, and what a commanding presence that illustrious man had. We briefly shared what Airline Ambassadors did helping vulnerable children, and in a booming voice he said,

"Feed my people!"

To be honest, it felt more like a command. Mandela introduced us to Bantu Holomisa, a General in the Transky Army, with whom we had an instant connection. (Dave and I both knew we had to follow-up on Mandela's order and later, with help from Monsanto, we provided locally grown seeds in an agricultural program that would impact 10,000 people. Graca, Mandela's wife, joined us on our trip to Mozambique, her homeland, where we provided donations of wheelchairs. It was all very touching.

Our next stop was Zimbabwe, where Ken had planned to deliver wheelchairs in the remote village of Mudze. This was a dangerous time in Zimbabwe, as President Robert Mugabe was taking land away from white landowners and giving it to the local workers. But workers had little idea how to run the farms, and deep racial trouble was brewing. It was many hours driving, so Ken was going to arrive by helicopter. A taxi took Dave and me on remote roads for what seemed like hours to that forsaken place. I had fallen asleep on Dave's shoulder in the back of the car when I suddenly felt a jolt and heard a loud thud. Our driver had accidently hit a girl.

I wasn't going to be held back by fear, so at the risk of starting a riot for helping a black girl, I jumped out to see how I could help her. She wasn't severely hurt, she still needed medical care, so we took her to the hospital. Although that put a bit of a distance between Ken's group and mine, as they felt my response could have jeopardized all of them, the truth is I'd do the same thing again, and my conscience was clear.

In July 2000, I received a letter from Armando Bukele Kattan of the Kiwanis Club El Salvador, officially inviting us to visit. Penny Rambacker, our MIA Regional Director, and I attended the Kiwanis International meeting to meet Armando and offer to bring an airplane to El Salvador.

I expected him to look Salvadoran, but he was of Palestinian descent and had grown up in El Salvador. He was a giant of a man in all respects, heavy set and jovial with a commanding presence. He had a brilliant mind and graduated in industrial chemistry from the University of El Salvador. A brilliant businessman, he had founded many companies in the textile industry, commerce, pharmaceuticals, advertising, and the media. His generosity and love for people transpired in his philanthropic work with Kiwanis, a community service institution that brought together entrepreneurs and professionals, much like the Rotary. Dedicated to Islam, he had founded the first mosque in El Salvador in 1992. He served as Imam of the Salvadoran Community, but had a much wider view of all religions and was also a founding member of the Council of Religions for Peace, with tolerance and appreciation for all faith traditions.

When someone pointed him out at the Kiwanis convention filled with thousands of participants, the first thing he did was give me a huge bear hug and I liked him instantly. Penny, Armando, and I went to a small coffee shop nearby so we could tell him of our plan.

"Now this is my treat; Kiwanis is not only about work, but about friendship too!" he said as we sat down.

We had sent a few missions to this country, but I had not yet visited there. I wanted to request the third airplane American Airlines was giving us to go to El Salvador. We knew that in Latin America, most kids received gifts from Papa Noel on Three Kings Day in early January rather than on Christmas. We suggested to Armando that our first airplane from American Airlines for 2001 be scheduled to El Salvador and we could fill it with gifts for children in different orphanages. He loved the idea and promised to coordinate logistics with five orphanages and transportation for our team.

"I'll handle everything from our side," he said. "I will work with the First Lady—Lourdes Rodriguez de Flores, and the Ministry of Foreign Relations to handle all the paperwork for the aid. You just need to send us an itemized list of who and what you are bringing."

"Will do," I said.

We shared a handshake, our eyes met, and we were bonded forever.

After the meeting with Armando, I called AA and formally requested an airplane to go to El Salvador in early January 2001 to deliver toys to orphans and vulnerable children on Three Kings Day. Gloria Reid, one of our best from DFW, had already volunteered to solicit toys and help lead the mission to El Salvador.

CHAPTER 13
ADVENTURES IN EL SALVADOR

Refugee camp in El Salvador

ON JANUARY 7, 2001, we took our second AA plane to El Salvador.

Prior to our trip, I called Patch Adams and offered to have him join us. Patch said yes, as well as all my best Airline Ambassadors: Leela Hansen, Elaine Osborne, Christina Andersen, Margaret Whitehead, Paula Latshaw, who also helped manage our escort program, Garry Flake and Richard, two of our LDS contacts—a total of 57 people. Armando Bukele and the Kiwanis Clubs of El Salvador would host the entire team.

William coordinated with LDS Charities, loaded the plane in Denver, and rode down on the airplane with the pilots to DFW. The plane first landed on the tarmac, near the hangar where Gloria Reid had gathered her boxes of toys. There were so many that they couldn't fit all of the aid on the plane. Gloria, of course, was furious. She had worked so hard to gather all this aid with love and devotion, and because I had asked William to load the plane in Denver, her donations could not all fit!

In the meantime, our team was in a festive mood, and even Bob Baker (the VP of American Airlines Operations, who had authorized our airplane), came out to say hello, giving me the chance to thank him. It's not professional protocol, but I couldn't help but reach out to give him a hug.

"Well Nancy, he said, right now is when people need support the most. American Airlines is glad to do our part."

He was truly one of the greats at American Airlines and I was very sad when he passed away at age 58. He was recognized as one of the industry's leaders, and even two US presidents had consulted him on matters of aviation.

When we boarded the plane, Gloria was sitting in first Class, her face red with anger.

"What's wrong?" I asked.

"Nancy, I told you to trust me. Your friend, William, filled the airplane with aid, and very little of the presents I painstakingly gathered for the kids fit on the plane. Why did you have to get involved? You should have let me just handle it!"

I truly felt terrible and asked William if he could take off some of the LDS aid and add Gloria's. But the plane had to leave so it could be back in DFW in seven hours. The plane was absolutely packed with every overhead bin and every seat filled to the brim. I didn't want everyone else to know about the faux pas with Gloria's aid, so I tried to be nice by checking in with everyone so rumors would not spread.

We landed in El Salvador and deplaned to the sweet, warm night air. Armando was standing there at Customs to greet us all, looking bigger than life. I introduced him to Dave, and they immediately hit it off.

Armando had arranged buses and a hotel for all 57 people for a four-night trip. Dave and I stayed at Crowne Plaza. To this day, that is still my favorite hotel, with a lovely view of the San Salvador volcano from the breakfast room and pool.

Armando had us start at the Catholic orphanage, Hogar del Nino Adalberto Guirola, where they had brought the aid from the airplane to decide how to divide it. I was amazed at how organized this place was despite accommodating over 100 children of all ages. The nuns had it running like clockwork.

Gloria was devastated again when reminded of how many of her donations were left behind. The aid was scheduled to arrive in the next few days, but when I tried to talk to her, she simply would not open up. I am the kind of person who simply can't stand it if someone is angry with me, so it truly put a damper on my spirit.

We were divided into five teams, and Gloria chose not to be on mine. I worked with Dave, Michaela, Garry and Roger Brown from LDS Charities, Leela, and Patch sitting amidst piles of LDS donations and dividing them up between each orphanage we were planning to visit. After a few hours, we were finished.

We separated out the donations for Guirola and our team gathered around. I made a formal presentation to the Mother Superior, explaining that more of the aid Gloria had gathered would come in the next few days.

We departed next to a lunch that Armando had arranged at Club Arabe, and AAI was presented with a *Diploma of Merit* signed by David Trejo, President of Kiwanis, and Carlos Herrera of American Airlines, who were both there to honor our whole team.

The next day, we distributed aid to two orphanages, "Instituto por Protectcion de Minor" and "Casa Hogar.'

Gloria had been coordinating with First Lady Flores ahead of time without letting me know. She announced on the bus ride home that the First Lady had invited our team to a reception that night at 6 p.m. She gave us the address, saying she would arrive early. It was lovely that the First Lady would do this, but Armando was in charge of our schedule, not Gloria.

I called Armando with the news as soon as I got back in the room.

"Senator David Humberto Trejo is President of Kiwanis El Salvador, who is hosting your visit, and he invited us to his home on the volcano at 7:30 p.m. He is leaving for Italy tomorrow, so we cannot miss his invitation," Armando said.

We were double booked! What were we supposed to do? We could not insult the First Lady or Senator Trejo. Somehow, we had to make it to both events.

I knocked on Gloria's door and called her room to no avail.

Armando had the bus pick us up and drive us to the First Lady's reception first, on the promise that we would be back on the bus at 7:00 p.m., as the drive to David Trejo's was quite long and treacherous.

I explained the situation to everyone on the bus, still having no idea how we could leave the reception on time, and gave them the option to stay if they could find a way back to their hotels. We arrived on time for the First Lady's elegant reception. They offered us *pupusas*, the traditional Salvadoran food, and some kind of fresh fruit watermelon punch, which was delicious. The First Lady, Lourdes Rodriguez, was not there herself; I believe that she was just trying to do something nice for us.

Among ourselves, we were asking how we were going to just disappear at 7:00 p.m. When Dave saw the African conga drum near the musicians, a light bulb went off in his head, and he asked the musicians if they knew Gloria Estefan's song, *Conga*. Luckily, they did and agreed to play it at exactly 7 p.m. We hatched a plan and Patch Adams agreed to lead a Conga line. We spread the word among our team that no matter where we were in the crowd, if you wanted to go to the David Trejo event, you would join the Conga line and Patch would lead you outside to board the bus.

Ultimately, 7 p.m. arrived, and Patch yelled out with his deep, resonant voice,

"Everybody, conga!"
Step, step, kick
Step, step, kick...

124

At least 20 of us got in line and conga'd out to the bus as Patch continued the chant. We were all laughing. Part of me felt horrible that we had left Gloria and some of our team behind, and I wondered what they were thinking now. If they had simply communicated with me earlier, this would never have happened. It was at least a half hour up to David's house on the San Salvador volcano, and Armando was planning to meet us there.

We went up a steep mountain and the bus driver pointed to a little path. As we turned the corner, I saw a beautiful cottage, like a Thomas Kinkaid painting, with candles flickering inside. We arrived first to a patio terrace filled with art and then knocked on the mahogany arch-shaped door, half expecting to meet a fairy tale character. David Humberto Trejo opened the door, a warm smile on his face. I had met him at lunch the day before, but as I took his hand I couldn't help but like him even more. Probably in his 50s, he was of medium height with sandy brown hair.

The house was furnished with antiques, filled with classical art on the walls, and lit softly in the warm candlelight. The scent of the candles and Bach's classical music floated through the rooms as he gave us a short tour of his eclectic home with lots of crosses, rosaries, Buddha statues, and other spiritual art and led us to an outdoor patio graced by classical sculptures, fountains, and manicured small pools with delicate flowers floating in them. The terrace offered a spectacular view of the mountains and the lights of the city.

David Trejo had grown up in Italy but spent most of his adult life in El Salvador and was part of the General Assembly, representing art and culture.

Armando invited us to the outside bar to have something to drink. (Being Muslim, he didn't drink but he knew the airline crews loved to party.) There was wine, beer, vodka, rum, and even Limoncello to choose from, as well as some juices, coke, and other mixers. I was ready for a glass of white wine to forget about leaving Gloria and part of our team. David was a consummate host and served delicious empanadas and other hors d'oeuvres.

When the clock struck 11 p.m., most of us didn't want to leave that magical and enchanting place. We reluctantly said goodbye as we had an 8 a.m. pick-up the next day for the two-hour ride to Ahuachepan.

Ahuachepan was the location of the last orphanage we were visiting—-it was a home for kids with HIV. One of our team members played Papa Noel and we distributed toys to all children—almost 70 of them. Elaine and I interviewed ten of them and had them write letters to their counterparts in the US.

For our last night, we went out again. I made another attempt at talking to Gloria, but she gave me the cold shoulder. I decided to give her more time. It was a bittersweet party, as most of the AAI team were leaving the next day on their own passes. Dave and I were staying two more days to visit with Armando.

He had invited us to lunch to meet his family. His wife, Olga, greeted us standing at the top of the stairs, looking like a goddess, with her long, curly abundant auburn locks and fair skin. But it was her beautiful posture and presence and the way she beamed at Armando whenever he spoke that gave me a new model of femininity. I wanted to be just like her. She was also an excellent cook and had prepared a delicious luncheon. Olga and Armando have four sons and a daughter, whom we met that day. Nayib (who knew he would be the future President), Karim, Ibrajim, Yusef, and a daughter, Yamille.

Armando took us to visit another orphanage in Apopa. The kids performed a darling song for us and the priest shared they needed $8,000 to replace the leaking roof on the facility. Dave raised his hand and said he would make a donation to replace it, and then Armando got involved in a bidding war and ultimately contributed $15,000 to that facility!

We ended the day at Armando's favorite restaurant, Las Olas. Dave and Armando hit it off, Dave admiring Armando for his brilliant intellect and breadth of knowledge on everything. As dinner was served, they got into a competition of who could eat the most oysters. I can't remember who won. All I can remember is how my sides hurt from laughing so much.

We had just been back in Burlingame a few days when, on January 13, 2001, I received a phone call from William Dise letting me know of a huge 7.6 earthquake in Santa Tecla, El Salvador.

"Nancy, this has got to be affecting the kids we just saw. Turn on the news."

I did and it was true. One victim described the damage:

"It was hard. It was heavy, and it left our country in shambles, literally on its knees. Complete towns fell to the ground hundreds of houses fell, walls crumbled, bricks and tiles flew. A landslide in Santa Tecla covered hundreds of houses, people, dogs, parakeets, bicycles, cars and trucks. And the people were running, screaming, wailing, calling their loved ones, screaming for help."

The reporter said that 63,000 houses were destroyed and 100,000 damaged. 500,000 people were left homeless. I called Armando immediately.

"Yes, come as soon as you can with help. Is there a way you can invite the President of Kiwanis International, Bo Shafer?" he said.

"Of course, Armando, and we were just on a trip to Africa with Randy Smoak, the President of the American Medical Association. I will invite him as well."

We set the mission for February 12th, a few weeks after the earthquake, to give us time to mobilize donations. I contacted Bo Shafer and Randy Smoak, and both agreed to join the team. William Dise contacted our friends from LDS Charities as well as Project Cure to get a donation of medical supplies from their warehouse in Denver. I called our El Salvador team and invited anyone who wanted to join us for a return trip. We mobilized a team of 11 people which included Dave, Michaela Maychowitz from our office, William Dise, Eileen Hudnal, Christina Andersen, Freddy Gomez, Earl Calleson, Bo Shafer, Randy Smoak, and two doctors, Mike Tolle and Dr. Arnold.

Armando was busy on his side too, and asked his 20-year-old son, Nayib, to have his PR company design billboard posters to welcome us back. (Who knew he was destined to be President!) He also set up a press conference at the Crowne Plaza, one month after the earthquake and invited Francisco Flores, the President of the country, to attend.

This time we did not have an airplane, but American Airlines authorized ten boxes for each member of our team, 110 in total. We arrived at midday and loaded the trucks with boxes of donations consisting of medical supplies, wheelchairs, hygiene kits, and other emergency supplies. A mile down the road from the airport, we spotted a huge billboard reading "United for the Children of the World" with the logos of Airline Ambassadors, Kiwanis Club, and the American Medical Association. It had been designed by the PR firm of Nayib Bukele. Who knew then that 19-year-old Nayib Bukele would become President of the country?

We then visited the Cafetelon Refugee Camp. The earthquake in Santa Tecla had left 500,000 people homeless and three refugee camps had been organized. Cafetelon was the largest; a community park transformed into a camp filled with thousands of tents. Right in the very center of the camp was another huge billboard, like the one we saw on the road to the airport, with all our logos. We took great pictures there and felt so honored by our support in El Salvador.

Dr. Mike Tolle and Dr. Arnold rushed to the medical center and immediately went into action. During the days we were there, they treated over 1,000 patients a day and identified 30 patients needing surgery. We made arrangements for them to come back down in March to operate at Bloom Hospital.

The rest of our team continued to see to the landslide in Santa Tecla where so many lost their lives. My heart was sickened by the pain people had endured.

The press conference was scheduled for February 13th, one month after the first earthquake. The goal was to highlight the efforts of Airline Ambassadors, Kiwanis, and the American Medical Association.

I showed up for the press conference. William started laughing when he saw me dressed in my navy blue and white polka dot dress with pearls—such an unusual outfit for me on a mission. I explained that it is not every day you get to meet the President of a country.

We sat at a long table to face the press, with me and Armando in the center, Randy Smoak and Bo Shafer to my right, and President Flores to the left.

Halfway through the press conference the table began to shake; another earthquake was happening. The room rattled and rolled, and a low sound like thunder permeated the atmosphere. Being from California, I had experienced earthquakes before, and I was not scared, but it seemed everyone else was terrified, especially the locals. Everyone got up and ran away.

"I know you are an expert in seismic technologies. I really want to have you check the Hospital Nacional de Ninos, "Benjamin Bloom," Armando asked Dave when the earth stopped shaking. It was the main children's hospital in El Salvador.

"Yes. When do you want to do it?"

Armando's eyes sparkled.

"How about now?"

The hospital had been refurbished in 1993, but when Dave checked for structural damage, he was worried about its stability.

"What about the babies? Are they ok?" I asked.

"Let's get them somewhere safe," Armando suggested.

Our team ran to the 6th floor of the hospital and, with the help of the nurses and hospital staff, ran with the tiny babies in our arms downstairs and out to a stronger one-story building nearby. We had grabbed a stash of the LDS newborn kits from the bus to put next to each child. The 20 little ones looked so cute in pastel blankets, totally unaware of their possible fate.

This sparked a huge effort from both Dave and Armando to modernize building codes in El Salvador and the US. For two years, Dave worked through Senator Dodd and the US Congress on bi-partisan legislation, while Armando worked with both Arena (right) and FMLN (left) parties. Their actions were successful in getting laws passed both in the US and El Salvador. The Construction and Safety Act of the Americas was signed into law in 2003.

Despite the earthquake, life went on, and, the next day, Bo Shafer and the Airline Ambassadors team dedicated a new Kiwanis-Airline Ambassadors clinic in the indigenous village of Santo Tomas. Freddy Gomez and Earl Calleson of the Wheelchair Foundation and AAI members launched a weekly TV show in San Salvador where wheelchairs were to be presented weekly to those in need.

I was inspired to write in one of our AAI newsletters:

"None of us can individually solve the complex global problems we face, but each of us can help at least one person. We can bring a jacket for an orphan that is cold. We can bring a blanket to a homeless person, deliver medical supplies to a clinic, or volunteer our skills, whether we are a doctor, builder, flight attendant, or a mother. Our effort may prove to be lifesaving for another human being. At the same time, we will experience that giving is more joyous than receiving. We will begin to shine with an inner light that will affect those around us and inspire them to also bring compassion into action.

Every major world movement has begun with the personal decision of a solitary individual. Will I use my energy and time to serve another, or will I not? Your support of Airline Ambassadors reflects your individual choice to serve. You are part of a movement that can spark a tidal wave of goodwill, unleashing creative potential unlike the world has seen. May your lives reflect the blessings you are bringing into the lives of others."

CHAPTER 14
9/11

A call to bring love into action

SEPTEMBER10, 2001. This day will forever be etched in my memory as the calm before the storm. What was meant to be a memorable trip to the vibrant City of New York turned into a profound experience that would forever shape my perspective on life, resilience, and the fragility of our world.

The skies were clear, and the sun was shining brightly, painting a smile on everybody's face, including mine, when I boarded my flight to New York. This was going to be such a good trip, and I was so ready to deliver my carefully crafted speech in front of a small group of First Ladies. Lourdes Rodríguez de Flores, the First Lady of El Salvador, had confirmed her participation and Sharrye Moore, the AAI representative at the United Nations, had booked the elegant Delegates Dining Room for the event.

As the plane reached its destination and the sunset painted the sky in sunflower orange and water lily purple, I couldn't help but marvel at the breathtaking view from my window. The city's iconic skyline came into view, with the towering Twin Towers proudly standing tall. They seemed invincible, a symbol of the strength and prosperity of our great nation. A day later, they would be reduced to rubble and the lives of thousands would be tragically lost.

Had I known, what would I have done differently? This question haunted me for months. As I flight attendant, was there any action I could have taken to prevent the tragedy?

But I didn't know. So I spent the evening with my dear friend Sharrye, at her apartment. She welcomed me with a big hug (she gives the best hugs ever; those types of hugs that lift the weight of your shoulders and the clouds of your heart), a delicious home-cooked pasta dinner, and a bottle of my favorite chianti red wine. Our conversation prolonged late into the night, meandering between family life and the latest shows on Broadway and the last-minute tweaks to our upcoming event to ensure the First Ladies will embrace our initiative to help vulnerable children.

The following morning, on the infamous September 11th, the distinct voice of a news anchor awakened me coming from then living room. Sharrye was a curious woman, always eager to stay informed about current events. The time displayed on my wristwatch was 8:30 am. With my event about to begin in a matter of hours, I had no time to spare. I took a shower, then started curling my hair as my friend was making coffee. From the open bathroom door, I had a view of the small TV screen where images were rapidly changing—people pulling food off the shelves in a supermarket, the busy alleys of Central Park, police officers riding horses.

Suddenly, a highly incongruous and surreal scene unfolded on the screen - a plane crashing into the first World Trade Center Tower. At first, we thought they were showing an ad for an upcoming movie, but the anchor's voice, grave and high-pitched, shattered our illusion. We'd just witnessed a terrorist attack.

"Oh, my God, Nancy! Those poor people!" Sharrye wailed. "What if they plan on wiping out the entire city?" she continued, her big brown eyes growing even bigger.

Those poor people...

The words echoed in my head, and then I pictured the faces of the passengers and flight attendants so in love with life—contorted with fear and reduced to a memory in the hearts of their dear ones. I wondered, had I been on one of those planes, would I have recognized the face of evil in time to stop it? Next, I thought about Dave and his love whispers waking me up in the morning and, for a second, I panicked. I, we, had to stay alive.

"We need to get water, have lots of water, just in case..." I mumbled.

Eventually, the shock subsided, and I realized it wasn't water I needed. We needed to get out there and help in every way we could. Everything in New York came to a standstill and Sharrye got word the United Nations was on lockdown. It was clear now there would be no meeting with the First Ladies.

I was sorry about the lost opportunity, but more consumed with how we could be of service to the poor souls struck by the tragedy that was unfolding right in front of us. We learned the Armory was a place that families were gathering and so we called and texted every AAI member we knew in New York to join us at the gather at 651 W 168th St. and decide together how we could best help. About ten of us gathered at that first meeting and we brainstormed: We could start with little things, such as giving coffee to a rescue worker, listening to a distraught family member, bringing a blanket to a child cold from the rain, until we figured out how to do the big things. Equally important, we needed to take the anguish, the suffering, and the hatred kindled by the media and channel it towards helping.

Over the next week, dozens of AAI members volunteered at the Armory, comforting families of victims, serving policemen and volunteers. Barbara McDonald became the darling of the soldiers, coordinated thousands of dollars' worth of donations, and was the first on our team to be escorted to Ground Zero, bringing coffee and comfort to the heroic relief workers. I will never forget my trip to Ground Zero a few days later, where the stench of dead bodies still permeated the air and smoke was still rising from the ashes. I called Dave in tears after my visit there and couldn't get the vivid images out of my mind. He said,

"You are there for a reason. Take that energy of anger and angst and turn it into love. Find a way, as you always say, to bring compassion into action. Not only will it help others, but it will help to heal your heart."

As always, he was right.

Within four days, Airline Ambassadors had 200 members certified to work with the Red Cross. I would run all day from one place to another, coordinating and helping. We connected with families who lost their beloved ones, and I learned all you could do was be there for them. Many others jumped in to support our initiatives. Hunter Public Relations, Smile Train, and UNIFEM provided radio donations and temporary office space. Esra Dogrameci and Cara Acker started our Adopt A Family Program, offering ongoing help to the victims' families. We distributed bright orange and black portable two-way radios amongst our core team so we could stay in touch.

I moved from one friend's home to another's, wearing one of my two dresses during the day and washing it in the evening, and having daily conversations with Dave. Even from miles away, he was my rock, and his voice soothed my anxiety and gave me strength even when I slept only a few hours a night. He encouraged me to keep helping and coming up with new ideas. I was motivated by the great love for our country and amazed to see the transformation of New York as the city completely changed amid disaster.

People no longer rushed to their daily affairs, blind to their surroundings. They were united in front of the deadly threat. Everyone was helping. Bus drivers would give rides for free to people who couldn't pay. Women distributed food in the streets. Shrines were set up in front of the buildings, with people's names and lit candles were burning. At 6 o'clock every night, a deep calm enveloped the city as everyone went into silence to honor the loss of innocent lives and the bravery of the first responders—unbeknownst to them, diving into a deep spiritual practice.

There was a silver lining in the horrendous events of 9/11after all—as there always is in everything we experience. The tragedy served as a wake-up call, reminding us of the deep bond we shared as human beings, a bond that is often forgotten during our fast-paced lives. The pain and suffering opened people's hearts like never before into an extraordinary outpouring of sharing and unconditional love. There was something truly wonderful about the feeling of genuine connection.

An entire nation remembered how to love more deeply in those days. But as I conversed with other flight attendants, I realized the same nation learned how to hate. Their heated conversations, dripping with anger and fear, would make my heart sink with sadness. Hate was not and it would never be the right tool for bringing peace and harmony on the planet.

I attended a meeting organized by the Association of Professional Flight Attendants (our flight attendant union) in Gramercy Park and seized the opportunity to say a few words.

"We can't channel this energy of the disaster into hate. Let's channel it into love and helping one another. The only thing necessary for the triumph of evil is for good men to do nothing or give into hate."

It seemed no one was interested, and I could feel the weight of my insecurities resurfacing, as if I was an outsider in a world that didn't understand me. I shrugged off the feeling and told myself that, regardless of others' thoughts, I had to stay true to my own path.

I'd seen that happening in my humanitarian missions around the world — lives crushed, communities decimated by poverty and disease, starving and abused children. So when 9/11 hit, I swore I wouldn't engulf myself in fear and anger.

`There were better things to be done with the pain and grief in our nation's heart as I eloquently shared in the post-attacks AAI newsletter:

"In New York, during the week following Sept 11, I had the same experience as I have had in the wake of other disasters: Hurricane Mitch, Kosovo and the earthquake in El Salvador. Despite the pain and suffering, people's hearts opened and the outpouring of sharing and unconditional love was extraordinary. Why must catastrophe be the catalyst for the appreciation of our oneness? This profound experience can be experienced daily if we would only take the time to help one another. When we bring love into action, we are in alignment with a higher part of ourselves. The result of that alignment is always...joy. As Airline Ambassadors, we build bridges of friendship between peoples and cultures.... we are Ambassadors of a new way of being. If we allow ourselves to be the crucible through which love can act. We are helping to build a new world and potentially a new civilization. Those of us in service are paving the way for a tidal wave of goodwill, unleashing creative potential unlike what the world has seen."

Nearly 3,000 people lost their lives on the fated day of September 9, 2001, including those on the planes and those on the ground. The attacks remain one of the deadliest acts of terrorism in modern history, forever etched in our collective memory.

It took flight attendants and passengers about a year to recover after 9/11 and not fear the plane they were on would be hijacked. Although deep down in my heart I knew I was protected, I became more cautious. I would scan each face in the cabin multiple times, monitor their moves and luggage, ready to report to the aircraft the captain anyone and anything that looked and acted suspicious. Luckily, it was never the case.

All airlines put in place new procedures that didn't allow passengers beyond the cockpit door. The Department of Homeland Security and the TSA were established. Remarkably, there has been no second occurrence of 9/11 until today.

The impact of witnessing the aftermath of 9/11 has shaped my life, serving as a constant reminder of the importance of harnessing the energy of hate and redirecting it towards constructive action.

CHAPTER 15
GIVING IS RECEIVING

With Maria Harrison, Leela Hansen, and Sharrye Moore

on a mission to Ecuador (left to right)

IT IS AMAZING that American Airlines gave us a third airplane in 2001 as 9-11 had just happened a month before. We dedicated this trip to Maria Harrison. Maria was the best Director of

Protocol Airline Ambassadors ever had! Born in Ecuador, she came to America to attend Averett University in Virginia. Later, she moved to New York. She worked at the Hospital for Special Surgery, ran a resource center for foreign languages at Beach Channel High School, and led numerous student trips as a Teacher/Leader for the "People To People Student Ambassadors Program." One of the first things she proudly showed me when I first visited her beautiful home was the souvenir spoons collection from each country where she traveled.

By the time Sharrye Moore introduced me to her, Maria was doing extensive volunteer work as an active member of the United Nations Women's Guild to raise funds for children in the US and abroad. I knew right away that she was one of us—those born to bring love into action—and had a huge heart.

Picture elegance and style combined with kindness and grit; green eyes that would tell a thousand stories just by looking at you and a radiant smile that would break open the most fearful hearts. Add a rare capacity to do everything to perfection, organize and connect people, whether it be First Ladies or abandoned children in orphanages. That was—and still is—-Maria Harrison, and to this day, we have a beautiful camaraderie.

Nobody could say no to this tiny (she only measures 5'3") unstoppable woman. When the tide seemed to turn against us, she always saved the day using some hidden superpower nobody would have guessed she had. Or maybe she simply knew what to say, how to say it, and when to say it. In a meeting with a First Lady or high dignitary at the UN, Maria displayed the class and poise of royalty. But when she delivered aid to kids, with her curly hair and playfulness, she became one of them.

In a way, Airline Ambassadors saved Maria. For she would never turn her back on someone in need, not even when grieving the loss of a child. On September 3, 2000, the unexpected death of her beloved youngest son, Robert Joseph Chindamo, took away the luster from her eyes. For weeks, Maria couldn't smile. She wouldn't answer the phone or leave her house in New York.

I remember calling her house to ask for her help with our mission to Quito, Ecuador. Initially, Maria said no. But when I offered to dedicate the mission to her departed son, she accepted. She knew he would have loved for her to do it.

Even now, when we talk on the phone, Maria will throw in, "If it weren't for that mission, I would have stayed locked inside forever. You brought me out of my shell."

Frank, her eldest son, immediately joined our efforts and offered to help with planning and logistics.

This was our biggest mission ever, with a 767 aircraft packed with wheelchairs, food, medical supplies, toys, clothing and 74 people. Among them, flight attendants, the widow of one of the pilots killed during the 9/11 tragedy, Debbie Sharpton, a TV crew from the Fox News Channel, and Inside Edition were there along with representatives of the Wheelchair Foundation, Medical Wings, and LDS Charities. The plane was filled with mostly aid, but there were still 74 people on board, and I spent most of the time checking in with each of them!

But the real challenge was to keep everybody together. I don't know how I could have pulled off this mission without Frank, Maria's son. Professor Frank Chindamo, a professor at Virtual Film School and the founder of LaughMD. His expertise in managing large groups of people as an Assistant Director while working on the set of blockbusters such as "Ghostbusters" came in handy. He didn't have a walkie-talkie to carry around, but he certainly knew what to do to get everything and everyone organized. "People didn't know me, so they took me seriously," he jokes to this day. Frank came up with a great plan, and I let him run the show as Chief of Operations.

Maria convinced all her friends to donate things they owned and didn't need. With the help of Maria Isabel Baquerizo de Noboa, the First Lady of Ecuador, she obtained permission to land the plane (otherwise, we would have had to pay a huge fee). Our team included two pilots and two co-pilots. One crew flew the plane in and then jumped into action with my team. We had only two hours to unload the plane, so the human chain technique was critical. We whisked everything off with just seconds to spare, and the crew of pilots and co-pilots did a turnaround and flew the plane back to Texas after just 119 minutes on the ground.

It was very important to get all the necessary permissions, otherwise our aid would have ended up confiscated or stolen. The big deal was to get the cargo in without hassle. But since the First Lady was involved in this mission, we didn't have to worry. Upon arrival, we were escorted into the VIP lounge while local volunteers gathered baggage, cleared Customs and placed the aid in the waiting Army trucks. Maria also convinced the managers of two orphanages to allow us to deposit the aid in two large rooms. She kept the keys to those rooms and promised to guard them with her life.

We had never had a mission as large as 74 volunteers, so logistically we were divided into three groups. The medical group was led by AA Cargo's Glenda Johnson (she later founded her own NGO - Medical Wings), the Mormons who would deliver aid from LDS Charities, the AAI flight attendants, and a representative from the Wheelchair Foundation to visit the orphanages and hospitals. Eventually, everybody got along very well and everything seemed to flow really nicely. It was harmonious and wonderful. Every day, we would deliver our gifts and visit projects until 3 p.m., and after, Maria would be our guide on sightseeing tours of Quito and its surroundings. For the dinners at night, Frank said he had to learn a new Spanish phrase: "Table for 74, please!"

With each hour gone by, I saw Maria becoming her old, lively self. Having Frank around was a balm to her soul. I surprised myself by stopping in my tracks and looking at them, captivated by a small gesture—-a shawl wrapped around her delicate shoulders, a hand holding the door open—-or a kind word. Maria, just like me, blossomed around children. There was so much love in her heart that, after showering her two sons with it, there was still plenty left. Looking back, the sweetest memories come to my mind.

Orphanages, as usual, were high on our list of priorities. Maria also took us to a special care facility run by Foundation ABEI Infantil, where kids from poor families came with their parents to get food, clothing and medicines.

It was during one of these visits that a young mother with her son came to us for help. With tears rolling down her cheeks, she implored, "Please help my son get a new eye." Diego Guzman had lost his eye to cancer at the age of 2. The prosthesis he had been using was too small and no longer fit. "The other kids at school have no compassion and make fun of him all the time," the mother lamented. "Please help us."

For a few seconds, Maria was out of words. I saw her jaw tightening, and I knew this moment was a painful reminder of her recent loss—- there was nothing she could do about it at that very moment. She could not battle cancer or death. But then her face brightened, and she said, "I will, I promise. I'll do my best."

What followed was two years of phone calls, letters, and downright begging until Maria had the good fortune of meeting Dr. Patricia Crespo. She, along with Dr. Steven Roser of Columbia Hospital, arranged for Diego to come to New York to be fitted with a new prosthesis. He was so handsome that they couldn't let him return to Ecuador without fixing his teeth problems. Maria took him to the barber and bought him sunglasses. In the picture she sent me, Diego, now 16, looked like a movie star. It brought his amazed mother to tears.

Our mission to Quito also took us to a maternity ward. Some of the mothers were so poor that they had to share one bed. The nurses asked us to leave the aid consisting of newborn kits, toys, and Beanie Babies with them, but Maria refused.

"Our mission is to deliver aid to people in need!" she exclaimed in a voice that left no room for argument.

She didn't tell those nurses that we were doing more than delivering "stuff." Maria knew that those mothers needed to feel loved, seen and appreciated. She hugged them and told them how beautiful and brave they were.

But hospitals and orphanages weren't the only places where children needed our help. The garbage dumps belonged on that list, too. Whole families lived in tiny derelict sheds at the dumps, and, as soon as the garbage trucks came in, residents, like ants, came out and climbed each new pile of trash in search of a meal or anything they could use to make their lives more bearable. When you see such poverty, you're no longer amazed that people can be so happy just to receive a pair of used jeans or a rain jacket. I remember Frank taking off his own T-shirt and giving it to one of the boys, touched by his suffering. Frank was no exhibitionist, so he was a bit embarrassed having to ride back to town with no shirt!

One of the most heart-wrenching yet endearing moments I experienced in Quito happened during a party for kids at Casa Hogar Santa Rita Children's Home. We were dancing with them and handing out Beanie Babies to the rhythms of each song. I noticed a beautiful little girl and handed her a bright red Beanie Baby but she reached up to show me—-I saw that both arms were cut off at the elbow.

She looked me directly in my eyes.

"Bring me my arms," she whispered, showing me the remains of her upper limbs.

Her name was Diana. Here I was, in Maria's shoes—-wishing I could do something on the spot. I gently set the Beanie Baby in her lap, but her request haunted me—-(inwardly I kept seeing her deep brown-black eyes and hearing her voice.) *Bring her arms? How in the world can I help this little girl,* I thought, and made an inner call for help.

As synchronicities go, a month after we returned home from Ecuador, I got a call from Maurice LeBlanc.

"Hello, he said, "I am a prosthetist and retiring soon. Does Airline Ambassadors have any need for prosthetic arms or legs or supplies which I would like to donate?" he asked.

"You have got to be kidding! Yes, and we need you, too ... What are you doing in March next year? I could provide you with a ticket to Ecuador!" I replied, still in shock (a good one).

"I might be available..."

Maurice showed up at the airport the following March looking tall and handsome with a great cowboy hat. He trained prosthetic doctors in Ecuador so they could serve other children as well, and also gave Diana back her arms with fingers instead of hooks (as were on many prosthetic devices.) The girl fulfilled her dream of becoming a drum majorette and was able to go to school—hoping to major in oceanography—-and even carried the Ecuadorian flag during a major procession.)

At the end of our mission and for the first time in months, Maria put on one of her favorite blouses, in vibrant blue, and danced at our farewell party. I knew she was finally on her path to healing. "This is what I want you to be," her son, Frank, exclaimed from across the dancing floor.

"It touched my heart," Maria remembers. "Life's worth living, no matter what."

Coming back through the MIA Airport, some of us had a few hours to wait for connecting flights, and I finally got a chance to sit down and have a long conversation with Frank, the dashing young man who had captured the heart of every single lady on the mission. Quite a few took me aside to inquire if he was single. No wonder; he was such fun to be around and had a hilarious sense of humor. I had no clue about his relationship status. But I could tell he was one of those men who enjoyed life and lived it to the fullest.

Frank confessed that the impression Maria had given of me had made me seem like some boss of a big organization.

"I figured I couldn't talk to you or anything. I'd just do what I can in the background to help my mom out. But then I saw you talking with people and laughing and smiling and I thought, "Maybe she's nice," he confessed.

He asked me why I founded Airline Ambassadors. I tried to give a short summary. Not a word was said except for the slurping of lemonade while I finished telling the story.

"Does anyone have your life rights?" Frank asked, looking at me seriously.

I started laughing.

"Life rights? What do you mean?"

"I think this would make a great book or movie!"

I've never said it before, but you wouldn't be holding this book in your hands if it weren't for that conversation. He helped me realize that my story would interest and possibly inspire people. I realize that, in telling my story, I'm also telling the stories of the many unsung heroes who built Airline Ambassadors International. Words are as powerful as actions when it comes to saving lives. And, by saving other people's lives, we save ourselves. As Maria Harrison selflessly says, "When you give, you receive, so you can give even more."

More visits followed to El Salvador, and one of them included Loretta Swit, our new celebrity spokesperson. Prior to that, the summer of 2001, we decided to change our headquarters to DFW where we had been donated a warehouse. Peg Meyer and Elaine Osborn agreed to run things from there, and later we hired Tara Dunn as Secretary and Eric Woodson as Executive Director to take the pressure off me.

Vitamin Angels had sent us a donation of vitamins and suggested bringing them to El Salvador. They wanted to be sure they had video documentation. This was another perfect opportunity to involve our celebrity spokesperson, Loretta Swit. She wasn't doing any movies or TV series and was free to join us on our April mission.

Knowing Nayib Bukele and his amazing public relations firm in El Salvador, I contacted Armando to see if he could help arrange an itinerary. He agreed. We had a great mission with Loretta and Nayib. His team filmed her giving a vitamin drink to kids at Guirola Orphanage and at Instituto de Protección del Menor. We also participated with the project, "Christ in the Streets", and supported hundreds of local youth in hand-delivering a warm and healthy meal to homeless individuals under bridges and in small clusters around the city. Nayib's team also edited and produced a short commercial starring Loretta. It turned out awesome and, as luck would have it, I had a perfect venue to showcase it.

Elaine Vaquilar of our New York team called me about an elegant Black Tie event at Oheka Castle in New York. She arranged for Airline Ambassadors to be one of the recipients and showcase our new commercial. Loretta Swit agreed to be a celebrity guest. Since we had just moved our office to DFW, I called them to make the arrangements for Loretta's ticket. In hindsight, I should have handled this one myself, as Loretta was bringing us her celebrity status and I would have booked her in First Class.

The day before the event, I received a call from her from the LAX airport furious that the staff had booked her on a coach ticket on American Airlines.

"I'm not going to fly in coach," she exclaimed "I thought you had me in First Class as your celebrity spokesperson!"

I spoke to the agent myself on the phone and begged her to put Loretta in First Class. They refused, and she was insulted and refused to board the flight.

I was embarrassed that she did not show up to our Black Tie Gala when we had advertised she would be there. We never got to use video footage or the commercial we had made in El Salvador either. Six of our AAI members did attend and it was a lovely food and wine tasting event, and I truly felt bad for Eileen Vaquilar from New York who had arranged the whole thing.

I'm grateful to Loretta to this day for her help and for paving the road for other celebrities to join forces with us. Actor Gary Sinise, Ken Behring of the Wheelchair Foundation, Lourdes Rodriguez Flores, First Lady of El Salvador, and Bishop Desmond Tutu, were some of the public figures that supported us throughout the years and gave credibility and promotion to our efforts.

I organized another mission to El Salvador that winter with Dr. Patch Adams. We visited the main Children's Hospital, Hospital Bloom, going room to room giving good cheer, toys, and gifts to children. As a token of appreciation, President Flores and the First Lady gave us the royal treatment at the Presidential Palace, handing us beautiful diplomas. Lourdes Flores (the First Lady) joined us on the visit to Instituto de Protección del Menor. I had seen it briefly on our trip in January, but this was the first time I really had a chance to look around. It was clean and lovely, housing about 100 well-behaved children. I'll never forget turning down a hallway and seeing about a dozen two year olds stark naked after their bath, their faces beaming with joy. As the nuns scuttled them away from us, obviously embarrassed that the kids had made it into the hallway, I asked the orphanage director,

"This place is just beautiful. What is your secret?"

"Well, it didn't used to be this way. Two years ago, this was dirty, dark, and a place of great despair."

"What happened?"

"It was you. It was the Airline Ambassadors."

"You have got to be kidding me!" I said. "We have had a few missions, but we have not raised any significant funds for you. How could teams of Airline Ambassadors bringing a few supplies and Beanie Babies for the kids have made such a dramatic difference?"

Her reply touched my heart deeply.

"It made all the difference. What mattered more than money was that you really care about us. The love that your teams brought inspired the whole staff, and they started cleaning up the place and caring more about the kids, whistling while they worked. Now the children are not dropping out of school anymore and stay off of drugs and booze. We are high on helping one another. Even the First Lady came to visit, and we are taking it forward with the kids by helping in the community."

This was what I had hoped would happen through Airline Ambassadors.

CHAPTER 16
KEEPING UP WITH THE NEW MILLENNIUM

Dr. Patch Adams escorting me at the National Caring Award

IN 2002, I received the National Caring Award. The ceremony took place in Washington, DC, and I was very honored that my dear friend, Dr. Patch Adams, introduced me. My wonderful supporters—my husband Dave, Annette Lantos, Aunt Mary Alice and Uncle David— joined me for this celebration. The evening wasn't without challenges.

Dave and I had brought our little Yorkie, Lulu, but the security agents adamantly refused to let the animal in. Poor Dave would have been stuck outside of the Ronald Reagan Building and International Trade Center with the dog if, in an amazing stroke of luck, my old friend, Mikhail Gorbachev, hadn't shown up. He agreed to carry our pet through the barrier. The guards relented and Lulu joined us too.

I had literally begged my Mom to be there, as it would have meant so much to me, but sadly, she refused as she had plans to see her sister. I offered to give them both a First Class ticket to join us, but Mom simply would not agree. I don't know why her approval meant so much to me and asked inwardly for the divine warmth of my soul to melt the frigid ice cube of my Mom's indifference. Although I was hurt, I tried to understand her and fill my heart with forgiveness.

Maybe she was sad that she did not use her own life for a higher purpose, and my success made her angry. Anger is a cover-up for hurt. She was doing the best she could as an insecure girl growing up in the '40s and '50s and maybe believed she did not have other options than to be a wife and mother. She had hoped I'd follow her example. In hindsight, my Mom was such an important teacher for me. She taught me tolerance, patience and detachment.

In January 2003, The Today Show featured Airline Ambassadors. Eleven of our members joined me in New York City. Additionally, Reader's Digest published a big story with a picture of me on the back cover. This prompted a call from Dr. Robert Muller, one of the men I had always idolized as a dynamic Under Secretary General of the United Nations. He agreed to join our Board of Advisors and told me he believed travel could play a fundamental role in building bridges of friendship between countries and cultures. Just what I had always thought!

Airline Ambassadors International continued to grow in the next years and bring love into action. We coordinated 75 humanitarian missions to directly hand deliver over six million dollars in humanitarian aid during our missions to Afghanistan, Belize, Bolivia, Brazil, China, Costa Rica, Dominican Republic, Ecuador, Guatemala, Haiti, Jamaica, Mexico, Nepal, Pakistan, Romania, Philippines, Senegal, Thailand, Tibet and Vietnam!

After the third plane to Ecuador, American Airlines stopped giving us airplanes. At first, I hoped it was a temporary decision, but as months went by, I realized I needed to come up with an alternative as it was getting tiring checking twelve to fifty bags per mission.

I was in New York for another UN meeting when an invitation popped into my inbox to a networking event where David Neeleman, the JetBlue Airways CEO and Founder, was the keynote speaker. I heard that JetBlue Airways was outsourcing their maintenance to TACA, based in El Salvador, where we had lots of contacts. I immediately confirmed my participation for the following day. I hoped that, since empty planes were flying there, he would donate one to Airline Ambassadors. My heart burst with joy as it always did when something wonderful was about to happen.

Red always made me feel more powerful, so I put on my lucky red suit and mentally rehearsed my speech during the cab ride to the location. I knew I would only have a few minutes—if lucky—to capture Neeleman's attention and set up a meeting where I could explain the full idea.

A born entrepreneur and marketing talent, Neeleman saw immediately the publicity potential in associating his brand with Airline Ambassadors since we were frequently in the news, on big TV networks, large-circulation magazines and newspapers, and would be a morale booster for his own employees. I think he also genuinely wanted to help.

He gave us a point person within JetBlue, and I appointed Cindy Paulus, one of our amazing members and a JetBlue flight attendant, as point person for Airline Ambassadors. For the whole initiative, Neeleman ultimately authorized seven airplanes, each carrying a load of 30,000 pounds of humanitarian aid, to bring support and relief to El Salvador, under the supervision of the new First Lady, Ana Ligia Mixco Sol de Saca. (Many years later, her husband would be accused of stealing money, but we had no idea what was going on behind the scenes.) All that mattered was that she cared for the children and was willing to facilitate our humanitarian work in her country. As beautiful as it was to rekindle the light of hope and joy in people's eyes, the formalities and paperwork leading to that moment were exhausting and draining. No humanitarian work is possible without the support of the local government and NGOs.

Before departing on each flight, we would have to send a list of exactly what aid we were delivering so that the First Lady's office could arrange for the proper Custom's clearances. We had already delivered airplanes of aid and were familiar with the requirements.

We planned the first mission for early 2005, and then another global tragedy unfolded.

On December 26th, 2004, Daniel Susott, our Medical Director, was snorkeling in South Thailand when the tsunami hit. The waves, the size of tall buildings, threw Daniel about like a feather in the wind. He managed to hold on to life for almost four hours. Exhausted, he made it to the shore, only to find utter devastation. At first he was shocked, but he then took action. A flamboyant character, Daniel jumped on the next plane to Sri Lanka, which had also been hit. He began coordinating with Dr. A.T. Ariyanee, a Nobel nominee, to help Airline Ambassador's efforts on the ground. Within days, we located 350 pallets of critically needed aid, water purification equipment, hygiene supplies, medical equipment, blankets, and food. Many thanks to Cathay Pacific and American for helping with transport, and especially to United Airlines for establishing a mileage bank for the public to donate United Miles for our work.

Daniel Susott wrote me from Sri Lanka:

> "Still happy to be alive, I like to think I played
> some small part in saving some of the 15,000 people

stranded in the worst-hit area of the southern coast. The bridges were destroyed, roads cut and 15,000 souls were marooned without food, clean water or even shelter. I called everyone I met from USAID leaving an urgent message saying that a fleet of helicopters was needed, and I learned tonight that they did indeed respond. I feel good about this. I did what I could, and maybe it helped."

Steve Ellis worked with the American Airlines flight attendant union (APFA) and helped organize an amazing Airline Ambassador mission to Thailand post-tsunami that was filmed by American Airlines. The volunteer team provided funding for fishing boats that were destroyed in the tsunami and helped by painting two boats and presenting them to the fishermen and their families. Through colleagues from Operation Playground, our team built a playground at a local school. They also provided school supplies and hand delivered more humanitarian aid for the people in Thailand affected by the huge tsunami wave.

The day before we were scheduled to leave on our first JetBlue airplane, I gave a talk in New York for about fifty people about the work AAI had done in the aftermath of the Tsunami in Thailand and Sri Lanka. It was followed by a party. I remember talking to one of the participants and, out of the blue, she said she lost her passport three times.

How could anyone do that? I had never lost mine, and it would never happen since I kept my passport safely in my wallet and with me at all times. Yet, who was frantically searching her purse for her passport the next day, an hour before our departure for El Salvador? Me!

Dave and I were in the cab the next morning on the way to JFK, and I just looked in my purse to make sure I had everything. I noticed the zipper in my favorite green eel-skin wallet was unzipped and my passport was missing. I looked at Dave in horror; we both knew perfectly well I couldn't check in for an international flight without a passport.

"I'm leading the mission. We have thirty-five participants, a full load of supplies, and Fantasy Flight (a pretend flight for 30 children of Kiwanis Village) with the brand new First Lady the next morning. How can I not go?" I wailed to Dave, sitting in the cab next to me.

"Calm down, honey! There might be a way," Dave said with one arched eyebrow and a twinkle in his eye. "I always carry a photocopy of both our passports in my suitcase. I have a copy. If I can distract the agent enough to get you on the plane, hopefully Armando Bukele can help get you into the country when we arrive."

The debate in my mind lasted only a few seconds.

"It's dangerous, but I will try."

I really needed to be there in the morning to meet Mrs. Ana Ligia de Saca.

Because this was the first flight of its kind, it was out of the ordinary, and that probably saved us. Maintenance flights were usually flown by the pilots, without passengers and luggage. However, on this flight there were 30,000 pounds of humanitarian cargo plus humans: Dave, me, Cindy Paulus, and 35 JetBlue employees.

Dave took the copy of my passport to the check-in desk, explaining that time was of the essence and that I had to go to Cargo because of an emergency with the aid. Fate and good karma must have been on our side because eventually the JetBlue check-in agent gave Dave a boarding pass for both of us. As I got on the plane, my heart was still pounding. We took our seats and Dave immediately called Armando Bukele.

"She's on," he said. "We are together on the flight, but please meet us at the airport because they may not let us in the country."

Armando promised to help, and Dave suggested that if anyone asked, the story would be that I lost my passport during our five-hour flight.

True to form, Armando met us at the Customs line. Dave and I were the last ones in line. He informed the crew he was going to give Dave and me a ride and told them to go ahead to the Crowne Plaza Hotel. Armando then introduced himself as a man of huge importance to the Customs agents and explained we had to be back at the airport the following day for a *Fantasy Flight* with the new First Lady Ana Ligia Saca and kids from Kiwanis Village, the village we had built after the earthquake in 2001. Armando walked and talked with an air of authority, and with his imposing looks, good nature, charm, and humor, had the agents laughing their heads off.

"Nancy is not going anywhere but back to the US unless you get her to the U.S. Embassy by 8:00 a.m. to arrange for a duplicate Emergency passport," the lead Customs agent demanded. Armando promised them he would see to it.

The Fantasy Flight was created to offer the underprivileged children from Kiwanis Village an unprecedented experience of boarding an airplane. The pilots that had ferried the flight down agreed to taxi the JetBlue plane around the runway while being attended by real flight attendants.

Sadly, I was at the Embassy during the beginning, so missed the new First Lady, Ana Ligia Mixco Sol de Saca, greeting each of the little passengers and taking their tickets. When I finally got to the airport with Dave and Armando, the plane was already on the runway and had to taxi back to the gate to add us as passengers.

The plane departed and continued to take off again down the runway. I helped serve a meal dressed in my flight-attendant uniform. At the end, the plane came back to the gate where Santa Claus waited and gave the kids presents. Their laughter, lively and merry like a crystal bell, still echoes in my mind. Back to Kiwanis Village, our team helped hand-deliver the aid we had brought, house to house. JetBlue had even donated $1,000 to buy gifts for the children. The group was given a reception at the U.S. Embassy, and their efforts were covered by every TV, radio, and newspaper in the country. I inwardly thanked God for my Christmas Miracle.

JetBlue authorized seven airplanes over the next two years, and Cindy Paulus, a JetBlue flight attendant, also fell in love with the Salvadoran people. She was a former flight attendant for President Bush and capably coordinated missions for JetBlue employees and Airline Ambassadors members, working closely with Cesar Calderon of the Ministry of Foreign Affairs. A humanitarian at heart, he became a great friend to both of us. Cesar facilitated paperwork, provided security, and also helped coordinate distributions.

A month or so later, after our first JetBlue mission, I learned that USAIR was also ferrying an airplane for maintenance to Grupo Taca. About the same time, Cesar Calederon was asking me to help hundreds of families living in the tiny hamlets and villages on the Honduran border. I decided to fly to Phoenix to meet with USAIR's headquarters. Doug Parker, the CEO of USAIR at the time, loved what we were doing with JetBlue. As we did a tour of the Phoenix airport, he agreed to fill the plane that was going down for maintenance with donated clothing and supplies!

Cindy had her hands full with JetBlue, so I led this mission. We ferried the USAIR airplane from Phoenix to San Salvador for a mission of only six people. Cesar had everything arranged for us. As I watched how he interacted with each community leader and set up a system with a loudspeaker so we could deliver big loads of aid to each individual family with love, I grew very fond of him.

Dave was not on this trip, but Dr. Daniel Sussot was. We loved having him, as he had an amazing and powerful voice. We would sing on the bus, sometimes together, and sometimes we would just listen to the soothing sound of his deep tenor. Daniel also had excellent IT skills, and every night he would show us a movie of the day's activities on his computer.

We were at a small hotel near the Honduran border sorting the mountains of clothing we had brought, separating women's, men's and children's clothing into separate bags. Daniel pulled out a bright purple satin dress, which was a rather large size. He held it up admiringly, then disappeared and reappeared in a few minutes wearing it. He handed me a tube of cherry red lipstick to apply to his lips. Then he began to sing and perform for us. We were all in stiches, laughing.

Throughout the first decade of the new millennium, Airline Ambassadors operated missions every month. Penny Rambacher opened her first school in Guatemala and dedicated it to her mom. We did a huge mission with NBC's Peter Greenberg to deliver beds to kids in Argentina. Sharrye Moore sent containers of aid to the Dominican Republic. Paula Moran delivered 100 hearing aids to Bolivia. Maria Harrison brought more aid to ABEI in Ecuador. Dee Roby organized balloon rides for orphans over Angor Wat in Cambodia. Deb Quigley opened a girls' wing at an orphanage in Bali, and Elaine Osborn led many missions to help Starbucks coffee farms in El Salvador.

Pretty soon, new celebrities heard about us and wanted to help. We supported actor Gary Sinise with Operation Iraqi Children. Singer Wyclef Jean joined Sharrye Moore on our mission to Haiti. This only increased our notoriety, and even more help came in.

We brought a team of doctors to Kiwanis Village in El Salvador, and William Dise coordinated a Holiday surprise for wounded U.S. warriors in Frankfurt, Germany, with the support of three vocalists from the USO and cheerleaders from the Dallas Mavericks (hockey) and Miami Heat (basketball) teams. We did clowning trips to Argentina, Colombia, Chile and Uruguay, and two of our members even got married on our mission to Cambodia. We continued to help the Hopi and Navajo reservations, painted houses in Trinidad, and gave gifts to orphans in Peru. We continued to send missions to the Philippines for our favorite orphanage - Shepherd of the Hills. We provided over a MILLION dollars of aid to Panama with support from Project Cure. We provided disaster relief to Chile, drinking water to villages in Nicaragua, regular donations to Haiti, and aid to orphanages in Jamaica.

We also established an annual prize for the Children's Medical Escort Program and, in 2004, held our first reception for the team in Dallas. Liz Wilson received the Margaret Whitehead Award. That year alone, our AAI volunteers escorted 143 children for life-changing medical care. American Airlines supported us by providing informational postcards that escorts could give to the pursers on their flights to acknowledge the program and alert passengers.

Soon after the Children's Escort Program reception in Dallas, Hurricane Katrina hit the southeastern United States with a heavy blow to New Orleans and surrounding areas. A Category 5 Atlantic hurricane, it caused more than 1,800 deaths and over $125 billion in damage, ranking at that time as the costliest tropical cyclone on record.

Dave's old Marine buddy, Frank Haines, from Sidell, Louisiana, called us to ask for our help. Their town was devastated, but his house was miraculously spared. He was married to a voluptuous Southern belle named Patty and had bought an entire ice rink and built a house around it. It was solidly built and we would be safe and he invited us to create a base camp there.

Our Airline Ambassadors Headquarters was in Dallas by that time, and our warehouse was full of aid. We had a strategy meeting with our headquarters team—Eric Woodson, Peg Meyer, Tara Dunn, Elaine Osborn and Kelly Lee. Kelly, an American Airlines flight attendant, originally from Baton Rouge, said she would help drive a van to Slidell and get her friend, Bob MCallan, to drive as well. Bob had been part of a chainsaw gang days after the disaster and was deeply moved to help. We agreed Dave and I would also rent three vans, load them up, and drive down in a caravan.

We had put the word out for support through all our networks, and on the drive down, I received a phone call that it was possible to deliver an 80,000-pound generator. We knew that power would be one of the things needed in this situation and organized for the generator to be delivered the next day to Frank's house in Slidell.

On the way into the city of New Orleans, a strong and handsome guy in a Green Beret Army uniform flagged us to a stop at the checkpoint into the city.

"Who are you, and what are you doing here? Are you from FEMA?" he boomed.

"No," Dave answered. "We're from Airline Ambassadors and are here to help you. The two vans behind us are with us."

"That's great! If you said you were from FEMA, I would have asked you to turn around and had the pleasure of shooting you in the back. Go on through!" he waved our caravan through the checkpoint.

The Green Beret Special Forces were being housed at the Audubon Park Golf Club and were basically running the city. Since Dave and Frank were ex-military Force Recon Marines, they were able to arrange a meeting. Guess who showed up?

The same guy who had stopped us coming into New Orleans. His name was Rob Byerly. It was decided that the generator could be best used downtown and Dave delivered it the next day to the Hotel Royal Sonesta so it could power the city and particularly the Charity Hospital nearby. Rob arranged some helicopter rides to view the aftermath of the damage and later married Julie, one of the volunteer doctors who had come to help. They asked Dave and I to be godparents of their first-born son, Jack.

We worked closely with the Emergency Operations Center and Louisiana State Hospital Association to effectively place dozens of volunteer and medical teams, using Slidell as a base. Frank and Patty Haines oversaw our relief efforts in the area and sheltered 10 to 30 homeless for months. Patty, as a true Mother Teresa, supervised the delivery of new clothing, shoes, hygiene products, and school supplies to thousands of needy families.

Another supporter, the Liz Claiborne Foundation, sent two million dollars' worth of designer outfits to New Orleans. The trucks delivered pallet loads to Frank's warehouse. Although a lot of humanitarian supplies were getting lost our aid was safe because his building, a former ice rink, was solidly built. There were lineups of women around the warehouse asking for clothing. It was hilarious to see so many women on the streets of Slidell wearing the same blue Liz Claiborne suit!

Every day we went out and helped families. Their homes were covered in mud, which we had to dig out. The people we helped touched our hearts, and by the time we left each home, we felt like we were part of the family.

Our teams learned that compassion comes in many forms. It's the physical cleanup, but equally, it's listening to people talk about their desperate situations. We did both, and we had fun in the process.

Elaine Osborn and her father, Fred, in partnership with Chefs for Humanity, helped arrange for the feeding of 3,000 people a day in Gulfport, Mississippi. They also distributed 475 turkeys for Thanksgiving and holiday baskets to families in Long Beach, Bay St. Louis, and Waveland. All volunteers were welcomed like family by those wonderful hard-working folks who were so grateful for our support.

Because we love animals, we set up a pet escort program. When Dave and I dropped off the van in New Orleans, we escorted two gorgeous Labrador retrievers on our flight back to San Francisco.

CHAPTER 17
PARTNERSHIPS

Press event with Congressman Tom Lantos
and his wife, Anette Lantos

2008 WAS A good year. Dr. Patch Adams; H.E. Inocencio Arias, Ambassador of Spain; Ken Behring, Founder of the Wheelchair Foundation; U.S. Congressman Tom Lantos; and Reverend Desmond M. Tutu, were on our International Board of Advisors.

Sometimes, when I looked at their names, I had to pinch myself to make sure I wasn't dreaming. Young Nancy, who'd tell her daddy she had a special mission on Earth, wouldn't have dreamed about meeting all these luminaries, let alone having them support her cause.

We had a big, fancy board meeting in New York City. When I presented a partnership agreement with American Airlines and UNICEF-USA, Peter Greenberg, a travel editor for NBC and *The Today Show*, voted against it. The contract stipulated that the flight attendants would raise money for UNICEF but no support would go towards Airline Ambassadors.

"Don't you see, Nancy? They are using you to get a relationship with American Airlines" he pointed out.

BUT, in my naiveté, I thought UNICEF was truly helping the kids and felt elated and proud to support them. I overruled Peter, and the Board agreed to sign the contract.

American Airlines, UNICEF-USA, and Airline Ambassadors would get equal branding, giving us a chance to inspire the public to bring love into action. This way, with an in-flight video, we could inspire the world.

At that same meeting, we also discussed creating an annual event for Airline Ambassadors, and I suggested we hosted a Compassion Ball at the United Nations to raise funding for our projects dealing with poverty, education, health, child welfare, and disaster relief.

The Board agreed and decided to pay $20,000 for a professional fundraiser to help. The event was set for June 19, 2008.

I used my networking skills to invite Ana Ligia de Saca, First Lady of El Salvador, as the Honorary Chair. The guest list included BanKi Moon, Secretary General of the United Nations; Ambassadors of the Dominican Republic, Ecuador, India and Vietnam; well-established journalists and celebrities: Kirstin Haglund, Miss America; Diane Tucker, Mrs. World; Dr. Patch Adams; and actress Olympia Dukakis.

The Compassion Ball was a huge success. I remember when Dave and I arrived at the UN Headquarters, a beautiful young woman volunteer offered to give me false eyelashes. In my excitement to get to the venue, I had forgotten to apply mascara and her keen eye had noticed. There was no time for beauty tweaks, though, as our guests were arriving in black limousines. Hopefully, my pale gold satin dress would draw their attention. Ban Ki-moon, Secretary General of the UN, rode the elevator up to meet us. I extended my hand in welcome and brought him to the photo area with all our logos in the background. Press celebrities Peter Greenberg, Ann Curry, and Harris Faulkner joined us for a quick photo.

We didn't hire an MC, as I was good at it and loved to entertain. As Dave took his seat at one of the round tables, I stood at the podium to welcome the crowd and give a quick overview of the purpose of the Compassion Ball: helping children, families, and communities in need. As the echo of my last words died out, everybody in the room stood up, clapping. I felt like an actress, winning her first Oscar.

The evening included entertainment and celebratory moments. Melky Jean, Wyclef Jean's sister, entertained us with her music, and we gave awards to William Dise, Eric Klein, the Lantos Foundation and LDS Charities. When the night was over, we counted $300,000 in donations. The sad thing was, when we paid all the expenses, only $30,000 was left to go to our projects throughout the world. I was appalled and made a decision inwardly to never again coordinate a special event where most of the money went to expenses and not the projects themselves.

A few months later, I brought Steve Ellis, Leela Hansen, Sharon Stein, Frank Campagna, and Christina Andersen, my best Airline Ambassadors representatives, on the mission to Peru, where we were kicking off the in-flight video project. UNICEF-USA said they would provide the T- shirts.

However, when we showed up on location for the filming, the T-shirts had only the American Airlines and UNICEF logos.

At first, I was astounded, but then I remembered Peter Greenberg's objection, "They are using you…"

Although it pains me to this day to admit, it was clear that UNICEF was using Airline Ambassadors to recruit flight attendants to voluntarily collect money for them in flight (our contract was actually with the fundraising arm for UNICEF-USA). Our fundamental difference in philosophy also became obvious. I believed that ordinary people could help those in developing countries, but UNICEF-USA did not want volunteers involved with any of their projects.

On a subsequent site visit to Chile, we met women that needed a kitchen facility costing $2,000. I ran it by our team, and we decided we could easily raise the money to help these women. But the UNICEF representative shattered our hopes.

"Never forget, you are here so we can film you helping the kids and have footage for the in-flight video and get more donations. Other than that, we do not want you involved at all with our projects," he said.

I don't know what angered me the most: his hostility or our hands being tied to give aid to those poor women we so badly wanted to help. A pacifist at heart, always seeing the good in everybody, I hoped they would eventually come around.

I remembered Peter Greenberg's objection, "They are using you…"

A year later, when UNICEF was focusing on Haiti and human trafficking, I suggested highlighting the pivotal work of Airline Ambassadors in that country building Safe Houses for trafficked children. The UNICEF-USA team said they were not interested in highlighting Airline Ambassadors humanitarian efforts. I knew right then and there that I had to end this partnership.

I guess some alliances work and some don't, and it's only when the heart and mind work together that one can make the right decision. And sometimes you just need to go through trial and error and take chances.

Luckily, UNICEF-USA was the exception to the rule. Airline Ambassadors International had spectacular and fulfilling partnerships throughout the years, but in retrospect, one of them stands out.

In 2009, we signed an MOU, Memorandum of Understanding, as a vital partner of the US military. It gave us more wings to fly and fulfill our missions.

Rob Byerly, the Green Beret we initially met during Katrina Relief, was stationed in Southern Colombia. If Airline Ambassadors could procure medical supplies and humanitarian aid and get them to his Homestead Air Base, he could get air transport. The U.S. *Plan Colombia* was to help the most important hospital in the area. General Pagan of the US Military Southern Command authorized the use of a C-130 airplane, and LDS Charities agreed to provide the needed hospital supplies and other aid.

Dave and I flew to Bogota, Colombia to board the C-130 to San Jose del Guaviare, our final destination. This place was the headquarters of the Revolutionary Armed Forces of Colombia, the largest rebel groups in the country. They had about 10,000 armed soldiers and thousands of supporters, largely drawn from Colombia's rural areas. However, there was a holdup. The American soldiers weren't happy at all about giving up one of their jump days to fly the C-130 to San Juan de Guaviere with hospital supplies and Beanie Babies for kids. But General Pagan took our side, as he could see the impact we were making. He realized Airline Ambassadors delivered more than aid; we delivered relationships and acted as a "force multiplier that had the power to win hearts and minds."

We had been waiting at the hotel for three days, and it was frustrating that the C-130 kept being delayed. We didn't know whether we had to wait a day or a week to make it to San Juan de Guaviere.

During the delay, we met with the First Lady of Colombia and the US Embassy to brief them on our plan. Susan Reichle, the US-AID Director, said that her agency would appreciate any help, but the Embassy would strongly discourage any US citizen to travel to that area, citing kidnapping and other worse scenarios that likely awaited. The U.S. Embassy could not be complicit in any part of potential danger to a U.S. citizen.

While waiting for Dave in our hotel lobby in Bogota, who walked in but my dear friend, Ambassador Lorenzo. I previously met him when I was in New York as the Ambassador to the UN from the Dominican Republic, and I just loved to be around him—he was always full of creative ideas. He invited me to join him on a diplomatic mission to Cartagena. Because I didn't know when or if the C-130 would be released...it could be days (or even weeks), I accepted his invitation. Dave, of course, had to stay with the plan and his role was critical in the successful delivery of aid with the military aircraft. I made a plan with Dave to meet up in Cartagena.

Wouldn't you know it? Just after we left Bogota, the clearance came through for the flight. Dave and Alex Restrepo, an American Airlines flight attendant and one of our mission leaders who actually commuted from Bogota, helped load the C130 with hospital supplies and flew in the cargo airplane on a night flight to San Juan de Guaviere.

Later on, Dave shared with me the details of their adventure. I could still kick myself for missing it.

Rob's entire Green Beret team was waiting, as promised, at the far end of the runway when he got off the plane. He was greeted by General Alvarado and Colonel Chavarro, from the anti-narcotico police, in a large black SUV with blackened windows. They were glad to facilitate AAI's plan to help the hospital, they said. Inside the SUV, Dave noticed another American sitting in the back seat. The man was about his age and politely offered to escort Dave to his meetings in San Jose. Dutifully agreeing, my husband instantly knew the gentleman in the back seat was his CIA overseer.

The crew drove Dave to his hotel while briefing him on the key people he would meet: the hospital director, the Mayor, and the Governor of del Guaviare.

Dave spent a week in one of the most dangerous places in the world and was lucky not to be kidnapped. He had arranged to rent a motorcycle, but his sixth sense told him to stay at the hotel. Later, he learned the FARC had already procured eight such victims they were holding at the airport. Dave would most likely have been the ninth.

When he finally joined me in Cartagena, I couldn't stop hugging him, as I felt fate had stepped in to save his life and was so very grateful. He had been in serious danger in Southern Colombia (part of me was sorry I missed it) but now I could finally relax, and together we enjoyed this historic and charming colonial city full of cobblestone streets, horse-drawn carriages, colorful restaurants and lots of music.

After we got home, we received an unexpected thank you note from General Pagan. The US military had been looking for a terrorist for years and was finally able to capture him because of Airline Ambassadors. This individual was one of the recipients of the school supplies on our flight and wrote the US military a thank you note for the aid from Airline Ambassadors. Where force had failed, kindness had succeeded.

CHAPTER 18
A NEW
MISSION

Little Somnang

2009 WAS A turning point in Airline Ambassadors Internation-al's history. It was also the year where I considered giving up my job as a flight attendant.

We had already built up a history and reputation as the only international aid and development organization to operate within the airline industry and act as a living link between world resources and world need. What made us—-and still makes us unique—-was the goodwill and friendships that evolved after help was given. Our structure allowed our members to make a personal difference in the global community by applying their unique interests and skills to helping others. In the last year of the first decade of the new millennium, we visited 19 countries, donated over 70,000 volunteer hours, escorted over 140 children and orphans for life-changing surgeries and to new homes, delivered over $1 million in aid, and did 27 humanitarian missions. It was during one of those missions that the idea of joining the battle against human trafficking bloomed.

We were preparing for a Mission Coordinator Training in Miami when I got a call from Deb Sigmund, founder of *Innocents at Risk*. She explained to me about the issue of human trafficking. I had never heard of it, but the fact that it was happening on airplanes had me invite her to our next Airline Ambassadors training taking place in Miami. They had to know about this heartbreaking issue and learn how to stop it. Deb was so dedicated to her cause, just like me, that she decided to miss a high school reunion to join us.

Every month I would take time off from my flight attendant job with American Airlines to go on a humanitarian mission. Just before the training in Miami, I flew to Thailand where we were providing beds for Hill Tribe children outside Bangkok. Peter Greenberg, still a member of the AAI Board of Directors, joined me as a special reward for our volunteers. It wasn't like they hung out all the time with the award-winning travel editor of The Today Show. One evening while we were having drinks at the bar of our hotel, he spoke about the Night Markets—places where tourism, sex, and commerce came together in a sickening combination. His voice was neutral, devoid of compassion or outrage as he described faces, types of body, gestures and actions—how you went up in a room where you got naked and then they covered you in soap—as if enslaving and selling women like cattle was in the natural order of things.

"Take me there, Peter. I need to see this," I asked him.

When he challenged me saying it can be dangerous, I reminded him I'd seen death in Macedonia. He finally agreed. No bullets flew in the air and no armed soldiers had us at gunpoint, yet Patpong Night Market oozed the same gut-wrenching energy. Everything that makes us human—kindness, dignity, sovereignty, love, our divine nature—was missing, taken over by base instincts. Girls from poor distant farms were being sold and forced into giving grotesque sex shows, such as smoking cigarettes and throwing ping pong balls with their vaginas.

As we trod among the avalanche of people, the girls pushed me for tips. Immediately after I opened my purse, they surrounded me, trying to snatch the money. For a second, I thought I wouldn't make it out in one piece. But as soon as the money was gone, they left me alone, their eyes prying for new faces.

The following month, I was with Dave and Alejandro Fernandez, another Board member, in the Dominican Republic on a mission to deliver educational and hygiene supplies. When Alejandro heard me telling stories about the Night Markets in Bangkok, he invited us to go to a brothel he knew, where I could talk to the girls.

"We'll have a couple of beers and leave," he promised.

The moment we walked in, the girls came on to me just as much as they came on to Alejandro and Dave. They were so desperate; it didn't matter that I was a woman. We ordered three beers and, as we sat there, I looked at the end of the bar and saw two guys sitting by themselves while all the other men in the rooms were covered with girls. That rang an alarm bell in my head.

Immediately after, one of them pointed at the door, looked directly at me, then slid his finger across his neck as if that was what he wanted to do to me. I ignored him and continued to talk to the girls in the friendliest possible manner.

One said she was in school, which seemed like a scripted answer, and was trying to make money to pay for it. When I looked down at the bar again, the same guy repeated the gesture not once, but twice, signaling that I was making conversation and delaying a sale. He clearly wanted to slit my throat.

My hands began to shake, and I set the beer down on the counter. We had to leave, which we did before even finishing our drinks.

As brutal as they were, both experiences opened my eyes about the realities of human trafficking and made me want to learn more so I could take a stand and stop it.

During the Mission Coordinator Training in Miami, Deb Sigmund briefed our forty members on the issue of human trafficking and shared the pamphlet she had created, emphasizing that many victims were trafficked on airplanes. Now that our people knew exactly what to keep an eye on, Airline Ambassadors was ready to jump in and fight this horrible plague.

However, fate has a twisted sense of humor. It was a coordinator who missed the training in Miami who really got us started on Airline Ambassadors' third major program. Her name was Deb Quigley, our Honolulu Regional Director, and she was leading a mission to Cambodia.

Deb and two other volunteers were walking down the road of a small village near Siem Riep when they saw a tiny girl standing naked on a dirt floor under a house on stilts. Poor thing, she was about two years old. She didn't have hair, and the delicate bones of her frame pushed against the skin of her shoulders and knees. Red marker traces covered her chest and legs as if she had tried to draw clothes on her own body, since she had none. "Her mother had abandoned her here, and we can't feed her. No one can feed her," the people in the hut above shouted.

The child was what the locals called a Karaoke Baby, the result of a young mother trapped into prostitution linked to the Karaoke bars that lined the village streets.

At first, she stared at the three white women, so neat and clean, like a frightened grimy animal. Deb was carrying an orange balloon (she always had balloons for kids) which she gave to the child. To her surprise, the little girl took it and then reached out her free hand and waved.

"Oh my God, we can't leave her," Deborah exclaimed, and her companions agreed. Deb took off her cardigan and wrapped it around the frail, young body. The infant no longer looked like a frightened wild creature but like a sweet child in need of love.

After a short debate, the group decided that the safest place for the girl was the nearby New Hope Clinic. Executive Director, Kerry Huntley, (a friend of Deb Quigley's) welcomed her and gave her a beautiful name, Somnang, which means New Hope or Lucky in the Cambodian language - Khemer. Later on, Kerry placed Somnang in a safe house with a kind housemother and eight brothers and sisters, vulnerable and abandoned.

Somnang's predicament reminded us of the over one million children who had been abducted into a life of slavery and prostitution. Many died at a very young age or grew up trapped in the same bleak situation as their mothers.

In 2009, Somnang's story started the third major program of Airline Ambassadors, Human Trafficking Awareness. As more and more of our members were briefed on what to look for, we realized that child trafficking was everywhere around us. I have many stories, yet two of them from the early stages of our Human Trafficking Awareness Program stand out.

Patty McPeak, the President of our Board at the time, called me from the airport in Atlanta, frantically sharing about a potential trafficking incident right in front of her eyes!

In the waiting lounge at the Santo Domingo airport, a man sat next to a cute little girl. Initially, Patty didn't think anything unusual was going on.

"Oh, that's such an adorable child. How old is she?" she inquired.

"I *think* she's two," the man replied.

"She looks more like a four-year-old. Where's her mother?"

"Lady, you ask a lot of questions," he snapped. "Would you watch my bag for a minute?"

"Sure, I can do that," she replied, not knowing what to do.

The man took the little girl by the hand and walked towards the restrooms. He came back carrying her. Patty freaked out because she realized he must have drugged the child. Then she took a deep breath and casually walked to the boarding desk.

"We might have a child trafficking situation," she said in a low voice to the Delta Airlines representatives and gave a slight nod in the man's direction. The woman behind the desk swallowed hard.

"What are we supposed to do? I mean, I don't know…"

"Tell the pilots to radio ahead to Atlanta Airport!", Patty answered. "And give this pamphlet to your flight attendants." It was the pamphlet from Innocents at Risk on human trafficking. Then she turned on her heels and returned to her seat in the waiting area before the man trafficking the girl became suspicious.

Patty watched carefully during deplaning and saw the man and little girl taken into a room for questioning.

"Good call!" exclaimed the Customs agent who checked Patty out. "This was, indeed, a case of child trafficking!"

The next day, Daniel Sheth, Sridhar Chillara, and six others flew out of Santo Domingo on JetBlue. We had all promised to be alert on our flights out. Sridhar noticed a woman, accompanied by a man, a little girl, and a boy, checking in for a flight. The adults were white, but the kids had the mocha skin of the Dominicans. The girl was crying, so Sridhar decided to talk to her. He dropped his passport as an excuse to bend down.

"What's the problem, honey? Are you ok?" he asked, but the white man immediately came over. One indicator of trafficking is that the victims are not allowed to speak for themselves.

"What are you doing? No, no, no. She's just upset because she's leaving her friends. We're going to New York City."

"Oh, you're going to New York City? That'll be a nice vacation."

"No, this will be a permanent move. These kids are staying," the man replied.

"You've got to take them to Canal Street. They will love this shopping area of New York."

"Never heard of it!"

Sridhar knew then and there the man was lying and possibly trafficking the children. He ran back to tell Daniel and the rest of the team of his suspicions.

The AAI team got in line behind the so-called "family" to the checkout counter and, to their surprise, the Customs agents were high-fiving each other.

"Yeah, those are the kids. Yeah. Yeah. We got them."

As they checked the paperwork, the man handed the kids to the woman who had bought the tickets (clearly an accomplice) and who was escorting the kids to New York.

Daniel and Sridhar kept close to the woman and children. In a friendly manner, Daniel asked where she was taking the kids. She said, Boston. An inconsistent story is another indicator of trafficking. Once they boarded the JetBlue flight, Daniel asked the flight attendants to check on the kids. They, too, noticed that things looked funny but didn't know what to do. The little boy had bruises on his arm and the girl was still crying. Daniel advised them to tell the pilots to radio ahead to Customs at JFK.

Our team got in line behind the trio when coming into New York. It appeared they went through normally. Daniel questioned the Customs agent about this, and despite the obvious signs of human trafficking, the Customs agents at the JFK airport let them go because they had all the paperwork correct, remarking that this could have been an inside job involving Customs agents in the Dominican Republic.

All they could do was to send an undercover agent to follow them to Boston. Later, we confirmed with International Customs Enforcement, and they busted a child pornography ring in Boston, saving 86 children in one day!

We had correctly identified trafficking on Delta and JetBlue and later that same month, AAI members identified trafficking on US-AIR and American Airlines as well.

If we could further educate and advocate on human trafficking awareness on our humanitarian missions, little girls like Somnang would never be abandoned by their mothers. Somebody had to give these children and women a voice, and since nobody else was doing it, it was going to be us.

CHAPTER 19
SAVING HAITI

Petra Hensley at the dedication of a safe house built by Dave Rivard in Haiti

JUST AS WE were realizing we needed to focus on the cause of human trafficking, another huge disaster hit the world. On January 12, 2010, a devastating earthquake struck Haiti, the poorest country in the Western Hemisphere, affecting almost three million people and inflicting another heavy blow on top of years of political, economic and social upheavals. Eighty percent of all the houses in the affected areas collapsed or became unsafe. Thousands of children lost their parents, and the majority of Port-au-Prince inhabitants ended up living in tents. Haiti was a one-of-a-kind special mission because we worked there for over two years. We coordinated the delivery of seventeen airplanes of aid, most of them non-commercial flights, filled with millions of dollars of food, water and medical supplies. We also implemented a large grant that took us all over the country.

Dave and I had traveled to Haiti a month before the disaster, bringing in an airplane full of aid. We were enchanted with the beauty of the land, a piece of Heaven on Earth, and the dedication of our local partners to change people's lives for the better. There was a ceremony to honor our team, headed by Bernadito Auza, the Catholic Nuncio in Haiti. After the ceremony, we went to dinner at Hotel Montana with the Nuncio and his friends; among them was the Archbishop of Port-au Prince, Joseph Serge Miot. We were talking about the natural disaster that had struck El Salvador and how Dave had helped save lives by passing the Construction and Safety Act of the America's (CASA Act) ensuring that every construction, old or new, was enhanced to resist earthquakes.

"We're safe from earthquakes here. We don't need prevention," the archbishop said, a grin on his face.

Ironically, the very thing he had disdained killed him shortly after. Archbishop Miot was killed when the force of the January earthquake threw him off the balcony of the papal nunciature at the Port-au-Prince Cathedral. Sadly, the Hotel Montana, where we had all sat together, also collapsed.

As the death toll after the earthquake went up minute-by-minute, Dave and I made multiple calls from our apartment in Northern California, trying to mobilize aid. I called American Airlines and begged them to lend us an airplane. I even had money to pay for the fuel due to a large donation from Sean Cononie of Miami Homeless Voice, a non-profit helping the homeless. Even the homeless were collecting money for the cause.

American Airlines outright refused to help us, so we ended up chartering an aircraft from Insel Air. I invited the Miami Homeless Voice to send a few representatives, as we were so grateful for their incredible support. Unfortunately, none of the beautiful souls that collected this money could join the trip because they didn't have passports, but they did volunteer to help load the flight with aid. Oprah Winfrey also sent a reporter and gave us a shout out on her show.

Daniel Sheth, our Board member, was on that first airplane filled to capacity with medical personnel and first responders. They rented a house at Delmas 33, near Port-au-Prince Airport, for Airline Ambassadors to use as a base of operations. We stayed there, meeting the airplanes and bringing in relief. Crazy things were happening all around.

One evening, one of Daniel's team saw a man and two women walking naked down the street. The local Haitians believed that if they walked naked, they could turn into werewolves and eat children at night. It had to do with their strong belief in Vodoo. A crowd, some swinging machetes, had gathered along the side of the road intending to kill them. If it wasn't for their swift intervention, the three *werewolves* would have ended up butchered and in a ditch.

January 15th, Dave hitched a ride on a military transport to Haiti, and I arrived on the United Flight accompanied by my dear friends Ruth Matranga, Deb Quigley, Daniel Sussot, and some journalists a few days later. Dave met me on the runway, and I was so proud of him for calling in the landing slots for Southern Command and coordinating airplanes for Airline Ambassadors. He looked so handsome, with the sun glistening in his blondish hair and a winning smile on his face.

" Welcome everyone," he said. "I've arranged transport for the medical supplies and the team of doctors to go directly to the hospital. Also, I can bring nine of you to the UN Logistics Center for a quick briefing."

The UN Logistics Center (LOG Center as it was known) was just being formed and very close to the airport. Tents were popping up everywhere for various organizations: UNICEF, the World Food

Program, Red Cross, Catholic Relief, Samaritan's Purse, International Organization for Migration, and many more. A medical center was also being set up. Dave gave us a brief tour so we could get the lay of the land and see the location where all the NGOs would meet every morning at 10 a.m.

As the sun began to dip below the horizon, we drove to St. Joseph's Hospital to deliver medical supplies. As we got closer, we could hear the distant moans of the patients echoing through the halls. The sound was haunting, sending shivers down our spines.

The scene resembled a spine-chilling horror movie. Thousands of people had been crushed in the earthquake, and it seemed all the survivors were here. They were stacked outside on cots throughout the lawn and some on the ground, their faces etched with shock, grief, and pain. The sight was overwhelming, with hundreds of people who desperately needed amputations to save their lives. The sound of screams and moans filled the air as surgeons worked frantically to save as many limbs as possible, without anesthesia. As patients waited their turn, knowing that without the surgery, gangrene would set in and kill them, the feeling of fear and desperation was palpable.

We comforted them as best we could. I remember sitting on a rickety chair beside a young man. Though I couldn't understand a word of Creole, the anguished expression etched on his face spoke volumes. The raucous noise of people shouting and wailing drowned out our sobs as we locked eyes, tears streaming down our faces. The surrounding chaos only emphasized the senselessness of the situation. I prayed for a miracle; something that would bring peace into his heart and restore his trust in life.

Back at Delmas 33 (the house that Daniel had rented for Airline Ambassadors) I first met the owner of the house, Pola Antoine. She was a beautiful woman who emanated peace and love, and she warmly welcomed us. She exuded an aura of calmness and contentment, like a gentle breeze on a warm summer day, and her eyes sparkled with a peaceful glow. Being near her made one feel at ease, as if all worries and fears were left behind. I could sense that she was completely at peace with herself and her life, radiating pure love and happiness.

As she showed us around the large house, she shared with us the story of how God had given her a message to open the house for volunteers after losing her husband a year before.

About thirty people were staying there that night, many of them sleeping on cots or with blankets on the floor. Dave and I were lucky to get a small bedroom—-another miracle.

The first night I was there, Dave woke me up around 2 a.m. Loud chanting came in from the open window, as if someone had placed a speaker at the end of the street. My husband's voice was calm, but lit by the bed stand lamp, his irises looked almost as large as the tip of my thumb.

"Nancy, they're coming after us. Get dressed. We need to leave, now."

"Oh my God, honey, do you think they're going to attack us? Because of the aid?" I asked calmly. I wasn't sensing any danger, but Dave still suffered from PTSD from his days in Vietnam and was alert to threat. Dave nodded and threw me one of his white T-shirts.

When we crept to the door we ran into Gael Antoine, Pola's son.

"Come outside….you have to hear this!" he said.

As we emerged from the house, we were greeted by the sight of a tent camp that was slowly expanding around the perimeter. The soft moonlight bathed everything in a silvery glow, casting long shadows across the grass. The air was cool and crisp, tinged with the faint scent of campfires burning in the distance. Dave's white T-shirt stood out like a beacon, its whiteness adding to the other-worldly illumination all around us.

We were spotted.

I could feel my pulse racing and my skin prickling with fear as we waited to see what would happen next.

But the locals had no intention to lynch us. They were praising and showing their gratitude to Airline Ambassadors for coming to their rescue. Our hands stretched towards the glowing moon, illuminating the dark night sky with its radiant light. A chorus of voices, both deep and high, joined in unison, resonating with grat-itude for the gift of life. The salty ocean breeze carried the sweet aroma of hibiscus and jasmine, mingling with the fresh scent of the sea. I felt a deep sense of awe and admiration for the Haitians, whose faces shone with sincerity and faithfulness. Their devotion to the moment was palpable, and I fell deeply in love with their unyielding spirit. I also made a silent vow—-to do everything in my power to help them.

The first thing to do was to find storage and plan a delivery strategy for the hundreds of pallets of medical supplies and humanitarian assistance building up all over the runway at the airport. We took what we could in trucks back to the house and thus our temporary residence at Delmas 33 became a storage unit for the new aid.

Meanwhile, Dave and I had our own challenges to face, and the biggest one was ... hunger. At Delmas 33, our breakfast comprised of just a pot of black coffee. The pleasant aroma of coffee beans filled the air each morning, but it wasn't enough to satisfy our growling stomachs. The sight of empty plates and the sound of rumbling bellies became a common occurrence. We were always left feeling hungry and unfulfilled.

Dave and I resorted to eating granola bars that came in on one of the airplanes, and, to this day, my husband can't eat another granola bar. Once those were gone, we had little to eat for days.

It was hunger that led us to Jean Paul.

One day, there was rice and beans at a roadside stand near the house, so we dashed there to get some food while it lasted. As we shoveled the warm food into our mouths with plastic spoons, the clinking of metal trays and the chatter of hungry patrons filled the air. Suddenly, a disheveled man appeared beside us, his eyes watery.

In a shaky voice, he introduced himself as Jean Paul.

"Please, please, help us," he begged. "My community needs water."

Unfortunately, we had already distributed all the water we had from the airplanes of aid. However, we thought that the UN Logistics Center should be able to find some. They had to!

We consoled Jean Paul and assured him we would provide him with the necessary water as soon as possible.

Dave and I strode down the bustling street towards the Center, our hearts buoyed by a sense of hope. We were eager to jump into action, but the response we received was lackluster. The administrator behind the desk instructed us to submit a written proposal for consideration.

How was it possible that no one seemed concerned or would respond to the immediate need?

Our disappointment was palpable as we turned to leave, the weight of the task ahead of us heavy on our shoulders.

Those people were going to die without water, so we had to act fast. The only solution we could come up with was to rush to the nearest store and buy a hundred bottles of water.

As soon as he saw us, Jean Paul's eyes lit up with a renewed sense of hope.

"We never thought you would come," he said.

The scorching sun beat down on us as we looked on at the group of people who were on the brink of death. Their parched lips were cracked and their skin sunburnt and dry.

Dave and I handed the bottles to the members of the community. We could feel their gratitude as we watched them gulp the life-saving liquid. An older woman hugged me so tight, as if she would never let me go.

It was the small NGOs, individuals, or the churches that did the most work, and not the big organizations like the Red Cross or the Clinton Foundation, as one might have expected. However, we had to work through the UN Logistics Center as, at least, it provided a communications center for NGOs.

Millions of dollars of aid were flowing to relief organizations. We submitted a grant proposal to build two new communities in Mirebelais, in partnership with Yves Prophet from the Global Vision Citadelle Ministries and Frere Armand of the Catholic Diocese for Hinch. Our vision was that, as we rebuilt, we would also train the Haitian workers in the US Building Code (using the CASA Manual).

Airline Ambassadors was the first on the ground in Haiti and first to apply. Rumor had it that we got the grant, however, we never received an official response. It turned out the Clinton Foundation got involved and took over all funding. We were advised to reapply with them, which we tried, but to no avail.

We had to find other ways to be of service. It was common for Haitian people in the poor sectors to give their children to the rich people in the towns. Those children are fed and put through school but have to work for the rich family like slaves. In Haiti, these children are called restaveks. As horrible as it sounds, they were the lucky ones. A more somber situation was living in the street. Yes, those kids had their freedom, but the police were hunting them like rabbits. Certain local NGOs, like Haitian Street Kids, did their best to help them. Michael Brewer, its founder, showed us horrible pictures of the police killing street kids, which he was trying to save.

During our first days in Haiti, families would come up to us, imploring us to take their children. Their eyes were filled with tears, and their voices cracked with desperation as they begged us to help. Some parents clutched their children tightly, as if afraid to let them go, while others held out their tiny hands towards us, as if offering them up for rescue. The weight of their emotions was palpable, and it was impossible not to feel the gravity of their situation. As a woman who loved children but wasn't blessed with the gift of motherhood, it gutted me that most Haitians would give up their offspring because they didn't want or couldn't take care of them. Since the orphanage situation could have quickly gotten out of hand, creating systems for the families to stay together was a better idea. I realized we could serve Haitians by creating daycare spaces for the kids so that parents could work; implement vocational training centers; and, overall, by encouraging families to stay together to circumvent the danger of entire communities falling apart and more children being brutally murdered.

Ruth Matranga, an adorable blond, hilariously funny, and with a heart as big as it gets, was instrumental in bringing our vision to life. She was a flight attendant and was staying with us at Delmas 33. One day, upon her arrival from a flight, she said in a excited voice,

"I brought two quarts of my special spaghetti because, guess what? Sean Penn is in town!" His organization, Community

Organized Relief Effort, has been named Camp Manager for the quickly growing tent camp in Petionville.

"We can share the spaghetti with him and introduce him to Michael Brewer."

"Oh honey, that's genius," I chirped and gave her a big hug. As hungry as I was, if that spaghetti was going to save lives, I was willing to let the movie star have it all.

Sean Penn turned out to be not only a phenomenal actor but also a fantastic human being, committed to helping others. Over our spaghetti dinner, he agreed to visit Michael Brewer and the children in Solino, one of the very worst slums in the world. We planned the outing for two days later. Penn and his colleagues visited Solino, providing medical care to those poor souls who were living like rats in a filthy cage. That evening, I saw Ruth riding on the back of a motorcycle with Bendy, a young black Haitian street kid who was part of Michael's tribe.

"I'm staying in the tent camp tonight, see you tomorrow," she yelled and flashed her winning smile. A few days later, she privately shared with me that she felt like she had a contract from a past life and owed some kind of a debt to Bendy. She ended up marrying him, although he was fourteen years her junior, to help him get a US visa. I guess there is nothing that love wouldn't do to be of assistance to the beloved.

Things weren't difficult only for the street kids. Penn's camp was facing pressing issues because of the lack of light at night. There were over 60,000 people gathered on the mountain. As night fell, men were jumping into the tents, trying to rape women.

Dave arranged for a planeload of batteries and flashlights and consigned the whole planeload for Sean. Both Dave and Sean were in this for the long haul and they became good friends.

Airline Ambassadors also stood out among the other foreign NGOs in Haiti by forging an alliance with the local police. Most people on the island were friendly and honest, but the rotten apples put us at risk each time we ventured to distribute supplies. It was easy for hundreds and thousands of people to fall into a crowd mentality, grabbing at every morsel of food or bottle of water we had. The police would ensure everything went smoothly when we received and delivered aid; in doing so, they had the benefit of looking good in their own communities. It was a brilliant move initiated by Dave. We applied for and received a grant for $1.5M from UNICEF and Minustah! Airline Ambassadors would enhance child protection through construction by rebuilding police stations to include Safe Houses for kids in seven communities: Port-au-Prince, Mirbelais, Belledere, Hinche, Miragoane, Cap Haitan, and LeCaye.

Trafficking had increased by 30% in Haiti after the earthquake, and there was simply no place to keep the children that were picked up by the police except in the filthy Haitian jails, sharing space with murderers and thieves.

The magnitude of our operations in Haiti required that Airline Ambassadors have a Country Director, and Dave agreed to take that position. He would have to put his environmental projects on the backburner, but he was up for a new adventure. He was the one with the construction experience, the new CASA program, and had masterminded our relationship with Southern Command and the police.

Ruth and Michael found us a new apartment in Petion-Ville, and we moved out of our location at Delmas 33. By that time, we had received seventeen airplanes of aid and distributed all of it. Dave now had to focus on building the safe houses and implementing the grant from UNICEF.

While Dave was focusing on building the safe houses and implementing the grant from UNICEF, I had to travel to the US to move us from the Bay Area to Washington, DC. Thus, I could work more closely with the Congress on the trafficking issue, which kept me awake at night. I also had to juggle commuting to Miami to fulfill my flight-attendant duties and going to Haiti every chance I could. I created most of those chances since, as a flight attendant, you can arrange your time the way you want. You can "drop" scheduled trips if you find someone to take your place or pick up trips if you need more money.

Dave stayed in Haiti for almost three years and recalls it as one of the happiest times in his life because he was living on the edge. All his friends from the UN Logistics Center had to be back inside after a 4 p.m. curfew, but not Dave; he would walk around the streets any time. Spearheading our NGO, he knew his role was to coordinate efforts and ensure that resources were being used effectively. The work took all his focus, physically (planning and building the structures), emotionally (dealing with personnel issues), and spiritually (as he had to rely on faith in the Great Creator for protection and guidance). He spent long hours in meetings and on conference calls with the Red Cross and other major NGOs, discussing logistics, assessing needs, and developing strategies for delivering aid to those who needed it most. He was constantly monitoring the situation on the ground, gathering information and analyzing data to make informed decisions. Despite the challenges and the long hours, he felt a sense of purpose and satisfaction in knowing that he was making a difference in people's lives.

Every time we met, the air was filled with the sweet aroma of love. The sight of each other was enough to light up the room with an intense passion that seemed to grow with each passing second. The sound of our voices was like music to our ears, and the feeling of being close to one another was like being wrapped in a warm, comforting blanket. It was like reliving a honeymoon all over again, every single time we got together. Despite our different paths, we shared a deep understanding and respect for each other's goals and aspirations. We knew that our love and support for one another was essential in achieving our dreams. We were each other's biggest cheerleaders, celebrating every success and offering comfort during the tough times. Together, we felt invincible and unstoppable. Our love story was not just about romance, but about two people coming together to uplift and inspire each other to reach their full potential.

I coordinated many missions during the next three years Airline Ambassadors operated in Haiti. Sometimes, while we have dinner on our patio watching the sunset, Dave and I recall those times with gratitude in our hearts for all the volunteers who helped us with a smile on our faces. Haiti tested our resilience, resourcefulness and faith many times. But we also had fun—-life is meant to be fun even when you're in service to others—-and learned how to adapt on the fly to unexpected situations.

One time, we brought singer Timmy Thomas to give a concert for the orphanage of our local partner, Global Citadelle Ministries. When Timmy was pouring his heart and soul into his famous song, "Why Can't We Live Together", as our team of 15 people were dancing in the audience with 120 orphans when the stage collapsed. No one was hurt, and we ended up laughing our heads off. To top it off, we had a flat tire going back to Port-au-Prince. Nothing goes as planned in Haiti!

Another case in point about plans not really working out in Haiti is the missing pancake mix.

We started a food program for those same kids, and we thought we could kick it off by making everyone pancakes for breakfast. I mobilized a donation of 100 pounds of pancake mix, but before our planned mission, I had to go to Dallas Fort Worth Airport for an Emergency Procedure Training (a once a year training for all flight attendants and pilots). I kept the donation with me as logistically it was easier. I checked a huge blue duffle bag full of pancake mix to DFW and lugged it to my hotel room that night. After the training, I brought the heavy 50-pound load back to the airport and checked it all the way to Port-au-Prince.

Upon my arrival in Haiti, I waited for the bag, and off came the duffel, but it was emptied of its contents. Customs might have thought it was heroin or cocaine. Either that, or they really loved pancakes.

We also organized a "Cruise for Haiti "with Royal Caribbean Cruises. We kicked it off with a concert in Miami before the ship departed for Haiti. The concert featured singer King Wawa, a Haitian American who had helped unload airplanes in the early days. We also had on display or sale a series of 12 paintings called "Moni's Kids" by Daggi Wallace, who was a flight attendant but also an amazing artist in her own right. She had joined me in

Haiti previously and painted the portraits of 12 children from New Life Orphanage.

Dave was completing his Safe House in Cap Haitian and had arranged to meet us when we came into port. We had loaded the ship with one ton of school supplies and hygiene kits and received special clearance from Royal Caribbean to have Dave pick up the cargo and go off-site to visit a local orphanage and school in Cap Haitian. Normally, when Royal Caribbean ports in Labadee, cruisers can leave the ship but not the compound that surrounds it. The compound hosts countless curio shops so cruise participants can buy local artifacts. I was so glad we got the clearance, as I wasn't interested in the curio shops and wanted the adventure of seeing more of the real Haiti and reconnecting with my husband.

However, as usual, nothing went as planned. It started when Daniel showed up at our welcome dinner in the Royal Caribbean dining room in full drag. Although it didn't bother me, my face turned red, as I had Annette Lantos and her children with me. They were proper Mormons, and I didn't want them to feel embarrassed as part of our AAI team. They were great sports about it, though, and participated in a fundraiser on the ship to raise money for the cause. Both Daniel and all the Lantos kids had incredible voices and were natural performers.

We were about to stop at the port of Labadee, and I was picking out my clothes to greet my husband when there was a knock on the door of my cabin. One of the crew handed me a note from the Captain.

"Due to the recent demonstrations (riots) in and around Cap Haitian, Royal Caribbean will have to rescind your request to leave the Labadee compound. Furthermore, the humanitarian supplies we have on board cannot be picked up today. We will leave them at the Labadee port for pickup tomorrow after the ship departs. I am sorry, but our commitment is to the safety of everyone on board."

"No!" I screamed. I had set up the Cruise for Haiti for this stop.

I frantically searched for the Captain, but to no avail. At last, I reached Dave by cell phone. He, too, had been contacted with the same news. He and one of his engineers were having the time of their lives in Cap Haitian, and I was sad to miss all the adventure, but there was no way to join them.

As the civil unrest in Haiti intensified in 2011 and 2012, protests and killings were happening every day, and people in our circles started being affected by it in tragic ways.

Among them, the Chief of the Bureau of Protection for Minors, a brilliant man, 32 years old, with a beautiful wife and two small children. He was researching a trafficking ring in Port-au-Prince, when a bullet in the back of his head prematurely ended his life.

Another colleague was killed while waiting in line at the bank.

Our banker's eight-year-old daughter was kidnapped. They cut off her fingers and did other terrible things to her. The locals were marching armed in the streets, and the situation was getting more dangerous every day.

However, Dave kept attending meetings, and he fearlessly walked in very dangerous areas with huge wads of cash in his wallet, as he had to pay the workers in each location while completing all seven Safe Houses and police stations throughout the country funded by the UNICEF grant.

My good friend, Annette Lantos, begged me to persuade him to leave Haiti before it was too late.

"You cannot tempt fate," she pleaded.

I knew only a miracle would do that. As much as Dave loved and still loves me, he would never abandon the cause he believed in. Nothing would scare him so badly; not after seeing death with his own eyes in Vietnam. I prayed day and night for him to stay alive in Haiti or to come back home.

By the grace of God, Dave listened to my pleas for him to return home and in June 2012, he boarded a plane for the US.

After months of spending more time apart than together, we were finally reunited. We had been counting down the days and planning every detail of our life together in our new home in Washington. I couldn't wait to feel Dave's arms around me again and to wake up every morning next to his smiling face. As I walked towards him at the airport, my heart was pounding with excitement and anticipation. When we finally embraced, it was like all the time apart had never happened. We spent the next few days catching up on everything we had missed and enjoying each other's company. Being with my husband was (still is) a magical and unforgettable experience.

Inspired by AAI's fight against human trafficking, and because he had witnessed its devastating effects himself, Dave decided to take a more active role in fighting this horrendous plague. To achieve his goal, he enrolled in school at the University of District of Columbia, specializing in Homeland Security studies.

CHAPTER 20
FIGHTING MODERN DAY SLAVERY

With Congressman Tom Lantos, and embassy official,
and Sandra Hodges in Kiev, Ukraine

SOME YEARS IN our lives are meant for harvesting; others, for planting the seeds for things that are going to transform our lives and, occasionally, the world. Actions and thoughts that seem random—-tiny gestures and big dreams; fortuitous encounters and unforeseen events—-sink into the fertile soil of our being only to germinate into something new that sprouts when the time is right.

When I look back, the year of 2010 was like that. You'd think that the situation in Haiti was taking up all our time and resources, but this couldn't be further away from the truth.

2010 was the year when Airline Ambassadors International brought one of the greatest human rights issues of our time to the airline industry and beyond by taking a public stand against modern-day slavery and developing a plan to fight against it. At that time, the numbers indicated that 100,000 to 300,000 domestic minors in the United States were annually forced into sexual slavery, and over 800,000 victims were trafficked across international borders. Many of those were transported on commercial air carriers. Yet, the general public and the governing bodies turned a blind eye to it. Correctly identifying human trafficking on four different flights in 2009 was a great start. But doing nothing else other than staying alert would have been like pulling out only a few weeds out of the hundreds suffocating a beautiful garden.

Luckily, where there is will there is always a way, and opportunities present themselves. In late March of 2010, I attended a briefing on human trafficking given by Congressman Chris Smith, author of the Trafficking Victims Protection Act. Two of our members, Deborah Sigmund (founder of Innocents at Risk) and flight attendant Sandi Hodges, were testifying. After the briefing, I followed the Congressman back to his office and blurted out:

"Congressman Smith, we have to get the word out to the airlines. Can you help us?" He seized me with his steel-blue eyes and kept silent for a few seconds, as if he was trying to figure out what to do. My stomach tied into a painful knot as the memory of other instances when my plea for help for our missions had been met with a frown and tight lips.

"I think I can. But you need to tell me everything and be absolutely honest," he said eventually, his gaze lightened by hope. This was exactly what I wanted. Talk to an official who was genuinely interested in learning the truth about human trafficking; at least, the truth we had learned by our own experience. I blurted out everything I knew. I told him about saving Somnang and identifying trafficking on Delta, JetBlue, USAIR, and American Airlines.

"It's not happening on one airline! All airlines are affected.

Traffickers use airborne transportation to move their victims from one continent to another. The problem is that the cabin crew members don't know how to handle those situations. However, the Federal Aviation Administration requires all flight attendants and pilots to take an Emergency Procedure Training every year. Infrastructure is in place to train all front-line personnel at no cost to the airline. What if we could use it to also train them in recognizing human trafficking? If our small team correctly identified trafficking on four different airlines, can you imagine what 300,000 eyes and ears could do? Thousands of lives could be spared," I concluded.

The congressman gazed at me thoughtfully, and I feared he thought I was nuts. I was wrong again, for he slammed his fist against his mahogany desk, and his thunderous voice filled the room, "You are absolutely right. Let's do this! We need two congressmen for a briefing. We can get James Oberstar, Chairman of the Transportation Committee involved. Meanwhile, start making lists of the contacts you have. We have to give airlines a chance to prepare, so the earliest I can do this is July 1st."

I was thrilled at his response and realized I had to spend more time in DC. As in… live there. Not only Dave loved the idea, but he encouraged me to move the AAI's headquarters to DC. It was the way to go forward if you truly wanted to fight human trafficking. I would have to live out of my suitcase—which was always ready and packed—-commuting often between our new residences, Miami, and Haiti, but this was old news. Plus, being married to a man as committed to bringing love into action as I was made me unstoppable.

From my base in Miami it was easy to hop a flight to Haiti so this would work. Despite being married and having our own place, I was used to living out of a suitcase.

Dave, my rock and my advisor, also suggested we hire an Executive Director for our non-profit.

But first things first; I had to put all my attention and efforts into the Congressional Briefing to Airlines. I made a list of my contacts at American Airlines, Delta, JetBlue, US Air, Spirit, and Frontier Airlines, where we had AAI members, and gave it to Congressman Smith's assistant. She added to my list prominent names such as; James Oberstar, Chair of the Committee on Transportation and Infrastructure, Amy O'Neill of the Office on Trafficking in Persons; and Laurel Smith from Customs and Border Protection. I suggested that we have a panel with me and two other AAI members to highlight the flight attendant initiative. The SA conference room was eventually reserved at the Congressional Visitors Center for public briefing on July 1, 2010.

As a flight attendant, I had to constantly update my physical manual with new Bulletins. Knowing the format, I wrote a sample Bulletin for American Airlines and printed copies in yellow (all Bulletins were in yellow) so that American Airlines or any other airline could copy it and just add their own logo. We also developed a one-page handout with facts on trafficking and which highlighted the stories of how flight attendants had correctly identified incidents on board. The day for the briefing came, and it could not have gone better. Laurie Curtis, the VP of Flight Service at American Airlines, had accepted the invitation, as well as representatives from ten other airlines.

Congressman Smith gave a warm welcome to the sixty people in the audience, which applauded him wholeheartedly. Laurie Curtis (Director of Flight Service at American Airlines) promised she would print the briefing I had drafted to go in the manuals of all AA flight attendants. Decision makers from Delta, JetBlue and Alaska airlines as well as the State Department, Department of Transportation, Customs and Border Protection pledged their help. I was on cloud nine and couldn't wait to have a spare moment and call Dave in Haiti and tell him about our victory and how AAI was making a difference in the aviation industry by combating human slavery.

The success of our briefing was like a good omen for moving back to DC; as if the city, with its clear blue sky and cool breeze rustling through the trees, was welcoming me back. I was glad to be back. Unlike New York, somehow this city always had my back. It was also the setting of many precious memories——the most precious of all, the blossoming of my romance with Dave. I couldn't wait for us to retrace our earlier steps and enjoy a buttery chardonnay in the patio garden of the Old Tabard Inn, our favorite restaurant.

Therefore, when I started my quest for an Executive Director and a space for our office, I expected the best.

Dave saw AAI as a big NGO and recommended Clarisse Conway for the position. As a Counterpart International employee, she had brought in some big grants. Her resume and references indicated she was the best candidate for that position, and after her successful interview with our Board of Directors, I hired her. A clause in her contract stipulated she would get an extra $5,000 if AAI broke her contract before its termination date. I was so excited to work with her that I ignored it, not knowing it would backfire sooner than expected.

We also found a small office for rent near 16th and K, just up from the White House, for only $900 per month. 1500 Mass Ave. was two blocks away, which was where I had previously lived. Two studio apartments were available there starting August 1, 2010, and I rented both; one for us and one for Lynette Widdison, who worked in our California office. She agreed to move to DC and manage our day-to-day operations. Lynette and I got busy furnishing our new apartments with donated furniture, and we did the same for the office. Clarisse and Lynette began working from the new space on 16th Street, and I made a plan to meet with them at least once a week, amidst my traveling for work and to Haiti. We set a telephone number of 866-ANGEL-86 so anyone could reach us, anytime.

Despite our first victory, there was so much work to be done. We had to continue to raise awareness and secure more support to be effective in our fight to combat human slavery. This modern-day plague called for regulation and legislation both at a national and international level. International organizations like the United Nations and our congressmen and senators, all located in Washington, had to acknowledge the magnitude of human trafficking and stop acting as if it didn't exist.

With the media busy covering political scandals, terrorism, the latest divorce in Hollywood, and politicians arguing about different bills, the silence shrouding the topic of human trafficking was deafening yet foretelling. It felt as if I traveled back in time, to the Earth Summit, where the participants indulged in the pleasures of the moment and ignored the bigger picture. The realization that we, as a human race, had forgotten about being interconnected as one saddened me. But sadness wouldn't help the victims. It was one of those situations where what was needed was focused and sustained action. If we weren't going to take action, nobody else would.

Airline Ambassadors was no longer a single woman with a dream; it had become the only independent relief organization of the airline industry. We had an impressive list of International Advisors, a Board of Directors, and thousands of volunteers and members. Human rights was one of the principles we stood for, and the rights of trafficking victims were being consistently violated. We had to shine a light on this issue.

In August, I received a call from Congressman Joe Pitts from Pennsylvania. He said he was impressed with what Congressman Smith had done a month earlier and, as a member of the Foreign Affairs Committee, wanted to coordinate a similar Briefing for Embassies. I immediately remembered him from our first event as the tall heavy-set Congressman with a shock of thick white hair and a lovely smile. Together we planned the briefing in New York for mid-September, much like the first one, with the same players but coordinated for embassies rather than airlines.

I called my old friend, Ambassador Lorenzo, the former Ambassador of the Dominican Republic to the UN, to make sure the Dominican Embassy participated. He confirmed and also hatched an incredible idea.

"The First Lady of the Dominican Republic, Margarita Cedeno de Fernandez, will be in New York for the opening of the United Nations. She is also committed to combating trafficking and is opening a portal called "Freedom Without Borders" that is to be announced at the United Nations. Why don't we give her a reception? We can host it at South-South News, near the UN headquarters, and even draft a memorandum of understanding, which we can sign at the event."

In case you're wondering what that is, a memorandum of understanding (MOU) is a nonbinding agreement that states each party's intention to take action and form a new partnership. The South-South News headquarters was outrageously elegant with a UN feel, with flags of all nations gracing the entry, and Ambassador Lorenzo was President. South South-South News was a media company (similar to CNN) dedicated to covering the stories of global development of government, private sector, and civil society.

"That's a brilliant idea! And we can even promote the event at our Congressional Briefing. It will give us even more credibility," I replied.

The Briefing to Embassies was set for September 21st, two days before the UN Reception. Congressman Pitts gave a hearty welcome to the fifty embassy representatives, and we used exactly the same format as in the former briefing. We shared the AAI success stories in correctly identifying human trafficking and emphasized it was happening in every country of the world. This time the handouts included an invitation to the reception at South-South News on September 23rd.

Dave and about thirty AAI members joined me in New York for the reception. We arrived early to review the Memorandum of Understanding that Ambassador Lorenzo had drafted, check on the catering, and make sure every little detail was in place. Alejandro Fernandez, a good friend of mine, had helped me enlist the help of Van Robert, a renowned painter, and had him do a painting on a human trafficking theme, which we would present to Margarita Cedeno de Fernandez. Alejandro's father, former President of the Dominican Republic, had been killed in 1982, and his brother and two cousins were well known in the fight for democracy in their country. We positioned the gorgeous 30 x 40" painting by Van Robert titled "Trafficantes de Innocencia—Smugglers of Innocence"— near the table where we would sign the MOU. Flags of all countries decorated the hallway to greet the guests when they got off the elevator on the 12th floor.

I remember how happy I was to have Leah Rivard, the daughter of Dave's brother, Bill, join us as she was now living in New York, and how proud I was to introduce Christina Andersen, who always looked so elegant, as our United Nations Representative to Yury Fedotov, the Executive Director of the United Nations Office on Drugs and Crime. We used the opportunity to do some interviews with important guests, which also gave content to South-South News.

When Margarita Cedeno de Fernandez, the First Lady of the Dominican Republic, arrived, Ambassador Lorenzo and I greeted her and made a short speech of welcome, lauding her for the launch of the Freedom Without Borders Online Portal. I shared the story of how we had identified trafficking on two flights out of the Dominican Republic. Both of us then signed the elegant MOU in both English and Spanish to collaborate on this fight against human slavery.

Then Alejandro graciously told her that he had commissioned the painting by a Dominican artist especially for her. She was delighted with Van Robert's abstract style of portraying a woman holding a baby next to a menacing trafficker. The reception was a big success.

My life was crazy, but I loved it. Somehow, it felt like I had two homes—one in the US and a second one in Haiti. And even when we were miles apart, Dave was always with me–in my heart and in my mind. I guess that's the beauty of sharing your life with a true partner or soul mate: you're always connected.

CHAPTER 21
LEARNING DETACHMENT

Reader's Digest
AMERICAN HEROES
Photographed by
Michael O'Neill

Could one woman, on her own, make a difference to thousands of children around the world? On the aircraft she travels in every day, Nancy Rivard found the answer.

SEE PAGE 21

My only media appearance without a smile

AS I STARED at my reflection in the dimly lit bathroom of my cramped Washington apartment, I couldn't help but notice how swollen my face looked. It wasn't just the poor light playing tricks on me this time. I could feel the puffiness under my fingers as I gently prodded at my cheeks. The thought of my 10 a.m. meeting with Clarisse, our Executive Director, had kept me up all night. She had been working with us for only two months and was already asking for a special bonus, although she had done nothing to deserve it. She hadn't sent the money we raised for Haiti, nor identified any grants, and missed doing basic tasks such as sending thank you letters when somebody donated to us. I could see the writing on the wall. Her request to work from home was the last straw. We had to have a conversation.

As I applied my makeup, my hands trembled with nervousness, and my mind raced to string the right words into sentences that would convey the message without hurting her feelings. I could hear the traffic outside, the honking of cars and the occasional screech of the brakes. The smell of freshly brewed coffee wafted through the air, mixed with the scent of my floral perfume. The mirror reflected my worried expression, and I could feel the tension building up in my chest as I prepared to have the difficult conversation. I'm not someone who enjoys being bossy or causing harm to others. The sight of someone being upset or hurt is enough to make my heart ache. I would much rather feel the warmth of kindness and compassion than the coldness of aggression and domination.

If Dave didn't encourage me, I would have waited longer.

"For Airline Ambassadors' sake, you have to let her go," he begged.

However, instead of plainly firing her, I decided to give her some options. We met at the office in the room we used for formal meetings.

"Clarisse, I'm going to give you a choice. You can work from home as you wish and make a commission on the grants you generate, or you'll have to change how you do things around here if you want to get your monthly pay," I said.

She threw me a furious glance.

"You dare question me?" Her face was turning purple red. "I am trying to get Airline Ambassadors positioned for the future. The thank you notes and other minor stuff like this is Lynette's job, not mine."

"You are her supervisor, Clarisse. If our day-to-day activities aren't happening, the buck stops with you. And where is the money we raised for Haiti?" I asked in a calm but firm voice.

"I pride myself on being completely transparent about money, and if Julie Manly raised this money, she has a right to determine where we give it."

"I don't think so…whatever is going on, it needs to stop. Let's face it, we're not a good fit."

Clarisse stood up in a rage, and her 5'8" frame seemed to be shaking.

"That is not up to you to decide. It's up to the Board, but if that's how you are running things, that's it! I quit!" she yelled and stormed out of the office.

To my surprise, I didn't feel remorse or regret. After all, her extraordinary performance had created a $50,000 debt to Haiti. With Clarisse out of the picture, I took the matter into my own hands and looked at our bank account.

Other than the money for Haiti, we also owed $7,000 for an audit for 2010 and $5,000 to Clarisse for ending our contract before its termination date. Add to that rent and salaries for our accountant and webmaster. The grand total amounted to $62,000.

I called an emergency meeting with the Board of Directors and begged everyone to chip in, but they shrugged in dismay. None of the people who had recommended her lifted a finger to help, making me question why they even had accepted to be part of the Board. The Board accepted Clarisse's resignation and also voted against having an audit for 2010. Dave was participating on the phone from Haiti and was absolutely furious. It was the only year in our history when we didn't have an audit. That was the bitter part of 2010—trusting people and being let down by them.

I borrowed $50,000 from my personal 401(k) account and gave it to Airline Ambassadors to cover the debt in Haiti and pay Clarisse off.

In hindsight, that was a bad move because it casts a bad light on the organization when the president makes a loan. But I always keep my word and am impeccable in dealing with others.

Not having an audit and me making a loan got us rated only a "3" on Charity Navigator that year.

It was a big, hot mess that taught me some great lessons in money management, which I apply to this day.

As an NGO, it's good to keep some money in the bank. I would spend every penny we received in donations for the project for which it was designated. Most non-profits take a 25-40% administrative fee. AAI did not. United Way notoriously gives a fraction of the funds they receive to the needy. (The rest goes to very high salaries for the people at the top.) But we weren't in it to make a profit or buy ourselves a mansion on the beach. I thought that the more I allowed money to circulate, the more came to us, enabling us to help people. However, I forgot about the administrative costs and having some money in reserve for the sustainability of Airline Ambassadors. But now I had to acknowledge that AAI operated within a defined system, and if we wanted to continue our work, we had to play by the rules, although they chipped at our authenticity and spontaneity. Oddly, the bigger we got, the more complicated things became.

I also decided that less was better and surrounded myself with fewer people; people I trusted and shared a similar vision with. Slowly but surely, the number of members of the Board of Directors shrank. They were elected for only two years, and when that time was over, I didn't ask them to stay. Few of them actually rose to the occasion, and, to this day, Dave Rivard, my dear husband, is the most dedicated member of our Board. When UNICEF finally paid him for the implementation of the grant in Haiti, he donated his entire salary of $24,000 to Airline Ambassadors.

The monetary challenge wasn't the only one I faced in 2010. My heart was filled with sadness. My soul craved peace. With Dave in Haiti full-time, I longed for the warmth of a real home and the joy of falling asleep in his arms every night. I longed for those early times of AAI, where I could go on every mission, look the people in the eye, and tell them words of encouragement and solace.

My life was always on fast-forward: I'd come to Miami from visiting Dave in Haiti, run to my flight and put on my uniform on the jet bridge, and then return to Washington and run to the office. I also attended meetings on the "Hill" (Congress) as often as I could.

I had little time to do the inner work I so much loved and needed for my inner balance. I missed being myself and being guided solely by my heart. I missed the old peaceful, merry Christmas celebrations.

My heart was telling me to go to Haiti and spend it with Dave and be his aid, as he was playing Santa Claus to the adorable children at the Global Citadelle Ministries Orphanage. But my sense of duty was stronger and pushed me to go to La Jolla, San Diego, to be with my mother and sister. It was what I had been doing since Daddy's transition on Christmas Eve, hoping for that sense of unity and love we had experienced when my father passed away to resurface. I guess deep down inside, I had always hoped Mother would finally realize the deep love and appreciation I had for her.

That particular Christmas ended up being the most dreadful holiday I've ever experienced. The once lively and vibrant house was now quiet and somber. The flickering lights on the tree seemed to mock me as they illuminated the room with their artificial glow. The atmosphere was suffocating, as if the walls themselves were closing in on me. It was a Christmas that I would never forget, though I wished with all my heart that I could.

At least I could talk to my husband on the phone. The atmosphere was tense whenever Dave was around. My mother's disapproval was palpable, as if it lingered in the air like a sour smell. Even my sister, who usually kept her opinions to herself, couldn't hide her disdain. The sound of their silence spoke volumes about their feelings towards him. They thought he exaggerated. Mother heard me on the phone shrieking with joy when Dave called from Haiti, and she would never miss a chance to make fun of me while Cheryl, my sister, would be right in there with her. Even though many years had passed since I resigned from my high-paying corporate job, my family still couldn't fathom my choice to live out of a suitcase like a gypsy for an organization such as Airline Ambassadors.

I had never felt so alone, so misunderstood, so out of place in my entire life–a stranger in my own skin.

Other than my long-distance phone calls with Dave, I would find solace and refuge in my favorite secret spot in La Jolla. It was a cliff over the ocean about half a mile away from Mother's house. I would gaze at the setting sun over the Pacific and take in the sky as it turned a soft blue and lavender. This was the place I had come nearly every night as a teenager to reflect. It made me feel closer to divinity, with the beautiful expanse of fields and daring cliffs perched above the ocean.

Was Airline Ambassadors worth so much pain and turmoil? My mind couldn't make a decision, so I called out deeply to God for help.

As He always does, God answered. Wendy, my old roommate, dropped by our house. We were both flight attendants and also shared a passion for spirituality. We had lost touch since I left for Hawaii, and here she was, out of the blue, with a bright smile on her face and a book in her hands. The title, embossed in golden letters on the dark blue cover, intrigued me. – "After you read this book, you could write the Master a letter," she suggested as she handed it to me. "I have been a student for many years. I think it will help you. It helped me." A pleasant current coursed through my body as I held *The Divine Teachings of Light and Sound* and read the name of the author, Sri Gary Olsen.

I knew about the Sound Current from my earlier esoteric studies. The AUM, or HU, is what Christianity calls the Holy Spirit. It is the Love that permeates and connects all creation. I was missing the Sound—that was the root of my unhappiness and doubt.

One chapter into the book, I knew I had found what my soul was looking for. Late at night, after Mother and Cheryl went to bed, I got the Florentine stationery from the big armoire in the entryway and poured my heart into my first letter to Sri Gary Olsen, founder of Master Path, asking to be accepted as a chela—a spiritual student. He granted my request. From that day forward, I began regular contemplation every morning as a continuation of my spiritual practice, which I had started in the mid-90's. To this day, I have never missed this sacred time. Contemplation allowed me to hear the voice of my higher self and get answers to my questions.

"No need to give up on Airline Ambassadors," she whispered … "Just deepen your awareness, and take all action in love with a higher level of consciousness and detachment."

Love, yes. Higher level of consciousness, yes. But detachment? I thought I was detached, but obviously I wasn't. Was I too attached to doing things my way and the results it brought? Was I attached to being in control?

The answer would reveal itself sooner than I expected.

CHAPTER 22
GROWING AWARENESS

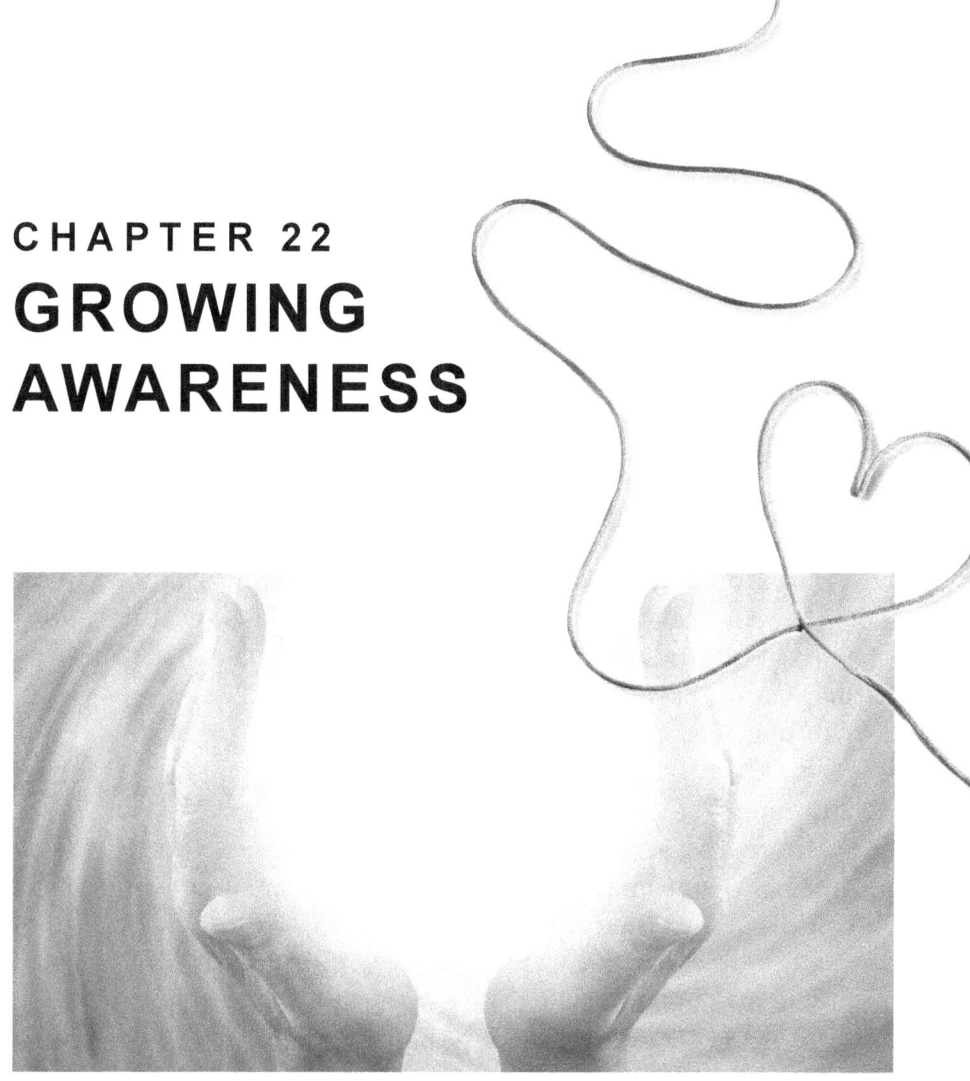

IN AN ATTEMPT to cut our 2010 losses, on January 1, 2011, and less than a year after we opened it, we closed the Washington office. I started handling all the thank you notes and the monthly updates. My life was still upside down with traveling, meetings, and more, but now I was at peace, for I practiced regular contemplation and reached up to God for guidance on every step I took.

A month later, AAI scored its first major victory. Together with the non-profit Traffick 911, we provided a free, six-hour training for flight crews at the Dallas Fort Worth Airport (DFW) a few days before the Super Bowl.

Using my flight attendant credentials, I secured a large conference room for sixty people, but there was standing room only as eighty people showed up! Dave and Renel Costumbre, Head of the Bureau for Protection of Minors in Haiti, joined us on that cold winter day.

Renel highlighted how trafficking had increased by 30% in his country after the earthquake and thanked Airline Ambassadors for building safe houses for kids. Traffick 911's team of professional trainers highlighted how trafficking increased prior to large sporting events, such as the Super Bowl, and warned that the flights coming into DFW would be packed with plenty of victims. I shared our story about rescuing many human trafficking victims on airplanes, and a heavy silence engulfed the room. I had written a press release about our training, and several of the press called American Airlines headquarters, who, unfortunately, acted as if they didn't know about it.

"Frank, why is American Airlines trying to put a damper on our training?", I asked Frank Campagna, a member of our Board at the time and an AA Base Manager in LAX. He was the only member of the airline who I could reach on the phone and was in a position to give us an honest answer.

"Nancy, how do I say this? American printed an article about Somnang in American Way last year to support your efforts. However, they don't want to take a public stand on human trafficking and risk the revenue coming in from the Super Bowl."

In other words, they didn't care about the young lives being broken and chose to bury their heads in the sand to make money. It wasn't the first time this was happening. It wouldn't be the last. The next month, when I attended my required Emergency Procedure Training, there was no mention of human trafficking. The Bulletin I had written for AA had expired and was replaced with a two-line sentence about human trafficking and the number to call if it was seen.

A question was lingering in big letters in the back of my mind. The briefings, the reception, the handouts, they were all great. But what had we really accomplished? The answer came in one of my morning contemplations.

"You're going to have to do it yourself. Keep educating and advocating."

In our Spring 2011 newsletter, I wrote,

"It will take all we have to give in time and energy, in patience, love and understanding. It will take our wisdom, and it will take lots and lots of money. This is our opportunity as humanity to build a social system based not on selfishness and competition, but on sharing, goodwill, and cooperation."

I knew this was also going to be the tip of the iceberg to shift consciousness about human trafficking. The Traffick 911's training prior to the Super Bowl had been a good one, but AAI needed something with its own branding, peer to peer, and tailored for the airlines. What was needed was an industry-specific, peer-to-peer training for human trafficking awareness, the first of its kind.

We spent most of 2011 developing just that, with airlines, airports and the travel industry as our primary audience in mind. Deb Quigley, the savior of little Somnang, and special agent Floy Turner, who trained law enforcement for Amber Alert and child protection, worked on the first draft. The three sections aimed at helping people understand the magnitude and background of human trafficking and its disastrous effect on the victims and, most importantly, identify signs of human trafficking and take appropriate action when reporting it.

In September 2011, we had a meeting at the DHS Headquarters with representatives of the Department of Transportation and Customs Border Protection to get their input. The training had to be compatible with the *Blue Lightning Protocol*, which is what Homeland Security called the protocol for airlines. After a few months of working \together and tweaking it, the training was approved. We presented it for the first time at the San Francisco International Airport Aviation Museum on March 12, 2012, with the help of Congresswoman Jackie Speier, who was representing San Francisco and the Bay Area.

The training couldn't be too long or we wouldn't get a crowd, so we kept it at 90 minutes and had four presenters. I would give an overview; Petra Hensley would describe the impact on victims; Deb Quigley would teach about the airline protocol; and Sandy

Dhuyvetter, one of our Board members, would highlight the importance of educating the travelers on human trafficking issues. Our promotion efforts paid off better than we anticipated. Not only did we end again with a standing room, but also CNN and local TV and newspapers covered the event.

Later the same month, AAI repeated the training to a full house at DCA Airport. These first training sessions became a launch pad for our third and newest program at Airline Ambassadors, which became our main focus for the next eight years. The presentation would be adapted and updated to fit the specifics of each city.

But in 2013, I realized this business model was faulty. I'll explain why.

First, the airport officials could pull the rug from our feet if they wanted. Case in point, the Airport in New Orleans tried to squash our event training at the last minute.

We had gone through all the right channels, including the Department of Transportation, to get permission to use the well-located airport press room, but when we got there an hour early to set up, I was notified that an emergency had come up, and they were moving us to the downstairs basement. That was such a lame excuse everybody could see right through it.

Some higher up at the airport received word of our training and, just like American Airlines before, didn't want to risk any bad publicity or revenue coming through that airport by highlighting the trafficking issue. The airport officials wanted the atmosphere to be, "Party! Party! Party!"

When life throws lemons at you, make lemonade. This is what we did. Dave stayed at the Press Room to redirect the participants to the new location while the rest of our team accompanied Anna Rodriguez of the Florida Coalition Against Trafficking, our guest of honor, to the new location. She was a force of nature, having brought the first case of trafficking to the United States as an attorney, providing training for the Organization of American States, and helping many countries pass laws on human trafficking. Laura Glading, the President of the Association of Professional Flight Attendants, also sent a representative to read her powerful statement.

At my suggestion, they became the first flight attendant union to sign the Transportation Leaders Against Human Trafficking Pledge.

Eighty people, including police and officials from Customs and Border Protection, attended our training—it was one of our best.

We couldn't continue to do this training for free and keep Airline Ambassadors afloat. After paying the hotel and flight bill for our team and for the marketing materials, we were left with an empty bank account. The flight attendants had to drop their flights to participate; we didn't want to exploit our survivor trainers by not paying them for their time, and no one from our Board of Directors would help.

At that time, AAI was being funded only by membership fees of $35 billed annually, with no grants on the horizon.

The only way for us to keep doing what we were doing was to charge $3,000 per domestic training or $5,000 for an international location. Thus, we covered the costs for implementing our Human Trafficking Awareness Program, paid the expenses for our volunteer trainers and survivors, and kept Airline Ambassadors sustainable.

The plan worked, and our first international training for flight crew took place in Kiev, Ukraine, at a meeting of the Organization for Security and Cooperation in Europe. We were later invited to Lyon, France, to present our experience to Interpol and did training sessions in London, Budapest, the Netherlands, Latvia, and Colombia. Airline Ambassadors was the first NGO to sign the ECPAT Code in 2014.

The demand for Human Trafficking Awareness training also increased in the US, and we were welcomed in Sacramento, Phoenix, Tampa, Chicago, Minneapolis, Las Vegas, Newark, and Dallas.

All this time, the Medical Escort Program was running on its own, and humanitarian missions were still going nearly every month.

My husband Dave invested himself into understanding the mechanisms of human trafficking beyond his academic studies. He was by my side at every training session we did and talked to the victims and the authorities. Animated by the same ardent will to save innocent lives as I was, he did everything in his power to combat this plague. He stopped traveling like carefree vacationers or busy business people do— their heads in the clouds or buried in their laptops. Instead, he would always be alert and scan the premises for potential signs of human trafficking. Eventually, this led to a major breakthrough.

While he was waiting at the gate for his flight in Philadelphia, a couple standing across from him in the same waiting area caught his eye. A New York flight was leaving thirty minutes earlier from the same gate. The dark skinned man was rather huge and burly compared to the young blond woman accompanying him. Her eyes were wide and darting around the room, searching for an escape. Her body was tense, and her hands trembled as she looked scared out of her wits. Sensing something off, Dave eavesdropped on their conversation—rather a monologue.

"Put your jacket on! We don't want anyone noticing those bruises on your arms," the man barked.

"When they call the flight to New York, you get on first, and I will be behind you and watching your every move ... Don't you ask for help, or you'll be sorry, bitch!"

The young girl, her body trembling with fear, hastily slipped into her jacket.

Dave snapped a picture with his phone, hoping he could relay this information to the LGA airport. As the flight to New York was called, he was on hold with the Department of Homeland Security Hotline.

"I have been trained to recognize potential human trafficking and have important intelligence," he explained to the agent when he finally got through. "I would like to get to LGA airport so we can have an agent meet flight 321. How can I text you the picture I just took? Time is of the essence!"

"We cannot accept pictures, but you are welcome to complete a police report," the agent replied. 'What was the man's name?"

"I don't know," Dave said, exasperated. "I have waited on hold so long that the flight has already departed!"

"If you don't have any specific information, we are not going to open a case on this," said the anonymous, uncaring voice on the phone.

Dave was furious and appalled that the Department of Homeland Security could not (or would not) receive pictures. When he later learned that this was the same case for Polaris, the National Human Trafficking Hotline and the Center for Missing and Exploited Children, he took the matter into his own hands. There was nothing he could do for the young woman on the flight to New York, but he was going to make sure things would be different in the future.

Although he didn't have a real technical background in IT, he used an Appy Pie (an on line program) to create the TIP Line App to report human trafficking. The app included many features. It had the latest news on human trafficking, a list of indicators, and a link to all 180 international tip lines in the world. Additionally, the app allowed the reporter to send a picture and or video and was fully encrypted, protecting both reporter and trafficking victims.

Early in 2016, Carol Palmer, representing the Ministry of Justice for the country of Jamaica, contacted me requesting AAI to provide several human trafficking awareness-training sessions for the tourism hubs in Kingston, Montego Bay, and the port of Ocho Rios. By that time, we were working with five human trafficking survivors, including; Donna Hubbard, who had the extra bonus of also being a flight attendant for American Airlines; Alicia Kozakeiwitz, specializing in youth; Shamere McKenzie, formerly of Shared Hope; Kathryn Griffiths from Houston Task Force; and Marcella Loaiza, who had been trafficked from Bogota and was bilingual.

We scheduled the trip for June 2016. Jamaica was rated a Tier 3 according to the US State Department's Trafficking in Persons Report, which meant that the government was not doing much to stop trafficking in the country. If a country dropped to Tier 4, there were serious trade consequences.

Dave and I traveled on passes on American Airlines through Miami and used them as stand-bys to save the miles for others. When flying stand-by, you never know what cabin you will get until the last minute, and we got lucky to be given seats in First Class. I introduced myself to the purser named Anna, explained what AAI was doing in Jamaica, and handed her a wallet card. The card had typical indicators of trafficking on the back:

Not being in control of their travel documents;

Under the control of a companion;

Frightened, ashamed or nervous;

Unsure of their destination and more.

"This may have never occurred to you, but as a flight attendant, you can save young lives. All you have to do is be vigilant, Anna …" I said. "Do you think you can do that?"

Anna took a quick glance at the card then slipped it in her pocket.

"Of course I can. And I want to. Count on me, I'm your girl!" emphasizing that all flight attendants had a duty to be vigilant to detect and discern potential trafficking on their flights.

The flight between Miami and Kingston is only an hour and fifty minutes, so the flight attendants are busier than usual trying to get the service done. Anna returned to her duties, although her open, wide eyes were telling me she had many questions. However, a little while later, she came up to me and whispered,

"We may have a case of trafficking in the coach cabin. Could you go back there and give us your assessment?"

"Of course!" I answered and immediately got up. I took my cell phone with me in case I could get a picture and made my way through the aisle.

The flight was packed, but I spotted them immediately—a young man in his thirties with longish brown hair, his arms covered in tattoos, and a thin girl, almost emaciated, sitting next to him. She had long dark hair, and her nails were over an inch long and shaped into a point, like daggers. I put my cell phone up and pretended to be looking at it, while I got a picture of the two of them, and continued to the back galley to confer with the other flight attendants. They told me she seemed under his control and he had her travel documents.

"When we see two indicators of trafficking, we have to take action and report this to the cockpit. Maybe we're wrong, but better safe than sorry," I suggested.

I returned to First Class and said the same thing to Anna, advising her to have the cockpit radio ahead to the authorities in Kingston.

As we taxied to a stop in Kingston, Anna informed me that undercover law enforcement would meet the flight. My heart was racing, thumping against my chest like a wild animal trying to escape its cage.

As soon as we stopped and opened the door, I ran out to meet them and show them the picture on my cell phone so they knew who to question. Dave and I stalled getting off the plane and hung out on the jet bridge when the couple deplaned so we could watch. Those two undercover agents could not have handled the situation more professionally.

They asked in a very unassuming way for the man and the girl to come for questioning to a private room near the Customs area. Later, we watched as they were released from the interview room and sent through Customs normally. We questioned the agent about what was going on, and he told us that their professional assessment was that this was not a trafficking case but rather a boyfriend and girlfriend.

I doubted their decision, but Dave cheered me up seeing the full half of the glass. The system we had put in place was working.

We shared this story during our training in Kingston, Montego Bay, and Ocho Rios. Our training was instrumental in moving Jamaica from Tier 3 to Tier 2 in the Trafficking in Persons Report. Later on, Jamaica became the first Caribbean nation to become a Blue Heart partner, pledging action to fight human slavery. That meant more lives saved.

CHAPTER 23
LIFE AFTER AMERICAN AIRLINES

Meeting Manuel...

IN 2016 I retired from American Airlines. It felt more like a graduation but without the ceremony, the flowers, and the acknowledgements. Upon my return to DC from my last flight to Barcelona, Spain, Dave waited for me at the airport.

We raved about being free to visit my humanitarian projects and make the best possible use of my unlimited flying benefits and started planning trips to the Philippines, Guatemala, and El Salvador.

The Philippines are one of the dearest countries to me because of Manuel. Not being able to give birth to my own child didn't mean I couldn't be a mother. When I first met nine-year-old Manuel in 2013, and he put the flower lei around my neck, I looked into his eyes, and we bonded instantly.

He had been brought to the orphanage at age four as he had seven siblings. They lived in a tiny tin house and their mother could not take care of them properly. When the Philippine social services contacted Shepherd of the Hills, they insisted that the orphanage take the kids. Originally, they were reluctant, but decided it was better for everyone to keep them together.

Manuel invited me to sit inside the little camping tent he had made and proudly shared about his brothers and sisters.

Years before, after my dad died, I had traveled to Sri Lanka to visit Dinesha, the little girl I had sponsored through Save the Children, but when they pulled out of the country, I lost track of her. I didn't want that to happen again with Manuel, so I suggested we start a sponsorship program for orphans. Christine Page, an American Airlines flight attendant, took me up on it. She was skilled, and took pictures, and wrote bios for each child. I was the very first sponsor, of course, to provide education for little Manuel. I'm so proud that we were able to get all fifty children at Shepherd of the Hills Orphanage sponsored, thus giving them the resources to go to school and change their lives forever. All of them were incredible with their own personalities. I couldn't wait for Dave to meet them, especially Manuel.

We planned a trip together for April 2016, over his birthday. On that trip, our team provided fifteen new bicycles for the children. I had previously bought one for Manuel, but since it was the only bike at the orphanage, and his heart was generous, he let everyone else use it.

Although it was past Easter, just for fun, we organized an egg hunt for the kids as an evening activity. Coins and candies were hidden inside each colorful plastic Easter egg, also wrapped in a strip of photo luminescent tape. The children were given toys to play with in the cafeteria while our team hid the eggs throughout the orphanage. As soon as we gave them the green light to search for them, shrieks of delight filled the air as children uncovered the eggs behind trees, in bicycle tires, and under the eaves.

Each child carried a small Easter basket to collect the treasures. Guess who collected the most eggs of all? Little Caleb, who had been blind since birth. His victory showed the deep spirituality embedded in the kids at this Christian-based orphanage. The leadership at Shepherd of the Hills Children Home has inspired them with a deep caring and concern for one another; therefore, all the kids shared their eggs with Caleb.

My husband, Dave, fit right in like a fish to water and behaved like a dad. He taught Maridel, Manuel's sister, how to swim. Every day was filled with fun. The children danced, sang, performed, and even surprised Dave with a special Birthday Party. He still says this was the best birthday of his entire life. Just like me, he wanted to stay connected with these beautiful souls and ended up sponsoring Maridel, Manuel's sister. We are also helping to put them through college, a lifelong dream come true to be a mom and dad together.

Besides visiting our humanitarian projects, I still worked as a trainer and organizer of our human trafficking awareness trainings internationally (Romania, El Salvador, Japan, Guatemala, Iceland) and locally (Anchorage, Chicago, Philadelphia, Las Vegas, Fresno, Dulles) as well as at all four of Air Asia's main bases--Manila, Kuala Lumpur, Jakarta, and Bangkok.

Our vast, significant experience helped to identify the key issues hindering the human trafficking movement: lack of an immediate response; lack of shared data; and the inability of law enforcement to receive photos and videos.

AAI solved this problem with the development of our TIP Line App. Data could come in in real time via airports throughout the world and was being deposited in an Interpol database. The next step was to engage an academic institution to analyze and share data with governments, NGOs, and civil society.

Originally, we pioneered this working with Georgia Tech University; however, despite our efforts to share this information, we could not garner interest. Since I surrendered my attachment via the morning contemplations, I decided not to push the river. If no one was opening the door, why push it? When the international community would be ready, they would act. Did I feel like pushing? Not at all.

Additionally, we provided a "Train the Trainer" program in 2016, but the problem was that the new trainers we had commissioned were happy to act as trainers as we were paying them a small stipend and covered their expenses, but it fell on me to actually sell nearly every training and negotiate all details. It was a lot of work, and I was running myself ragged. I just wished to find refuge in Dave's arms.

Don't push, my inner voice said in my morning contemplations. *If you don't like doing something, it's because you are not meant to do it. Relax and watch the show. Sit in quiet repose, and know that all is unfolding in the perfect timing.*

I surrendered and let things unfold.

It was in 2018 that I received an unexpected call late at night. Connie Rumbaut was an Airline Ambassador member and Executive Assistant to the American Airlines Managing Director for Miami. It was about Vanessa, the teenage daughter of one of her friends. Vanessa was volunteering at the Customs Border Security facility on 1st Avenue in Miami. There, she met Marlon, another 16-year-old from Honduras. Because he was very good looking and strong, his mother was concerned about him getting recruited by the "maras," the gangs so prevalent in Honduras. She had scraped together every penny she could to pay a "coyote" to get him to the U.S., where she hoped he would have a better future. The man did get Marlon to the U.S., where he was picked up by Customs and Border Protection and kept with many other kids at the facility on 1st Street. Vanessa and Marlon had hit it off as they were both from Honduras and the same age. A month ago, Marlon had been sent to a facility in Baltimore, and the case managers had placed him with the coyote because he had claimed he was a friend of the family.

Connie paused for a second and, after a deep sigh, she continued her story.

The day before, Vanessa got a Facebook message from Marlon, saying the coyote told him he was in debt bondage. He had to earn money to pay back the $10,000 he owed. When the man made sexual moves on him, Marlon decided to run away. Vanessa begged him to wait until she could get there. The girl left for DC on Connie's passes and was about to land in five minutes in Washington and then meet Marlon at the bus station in Baltimore.

My heart was pounding in my chest, and my mind was racing. I asked Connie to text me Vanessa's picture and advised her to call the DHS and Polaris Hotlines.

I rushed to the airport, left my little green Mistubushi running at the curb, and ran in to check the flights. Unfortunately, Vanessa's flight had arrived early. I didn't have her cell and had no other way to reach her. She had probably left in a taxi or Uber. She would need at least an hour to get to the bus station in Baltimore to meet Marlon, which bought me time to come up with something. But with what?

I decided to call Greg Bristol, a retired FBI agent, very good at his job. He had put together a training on human trafficking for law enforcement officials and we had presented together at the UNODC meeting in Vienna. Sitting in my car, I called his cell.

"Greg, we have a situation here, and I need help."

I shared the story and gave him the address of the bus station in Baltimore where Marlon was meeting Vanessa.

"You are in Towson, and it's much closer to Baltimore, so we have to move fast. Do you think I should go with you?"

"No," he said, "This situation could be very dangerous, as Freddy Lopez is probably looking for Marlon, and it is nearly midnight." Freddy Lopez was the *coyote*'s name (a coyote is what they call the trafficker). "I'm jumping in the car now and taking Lucky with me." Lucky was Greg's dog and trained as a police dog and service animal.

"The best thing you can do is call the DHS Hotline and Polaris and give them all the information you just gave me."

I went home and did just that and encouraged both DHS and Polaris to take action. Just after midnight, I called Connie back.

"Connie, I am going crazy as I have no way of reaching Vanessa."

"Me neither, but she left a message a little while ago that she made a reservation at the Roadway Inn in Woodland. However, I don't have her cell phone, either, and no way to reach her."

"Please, keep me posted," I said and then immediately relayed the information to Greg. He was at the bus station, but no one was there.

"It kills me that this trafficker, Freddy Lopez, extorted $5,000 from Marlon's mom and is now posing as a "foster parent" friend of the family, so he can get another $1,000 a month from Health and Human Services," he said in a pained voice. "No doubt he'll now try to traffic him for sex. I'm on my way to the Inn now. Marlon may have been able to get out of the house without Freddy knowing; the kid is street smart, I'm sure. I don't want to scare them, but I will scan the scene and be there to protect them should they need it until law enforcement arrives." As soon as we hung up, I called DHS and Polaris to update them as well.

I did that and didn't sleep a wink that night, tossing and turning in my bed. Early in the morning, there was still no sign of the runaway teenagers. Greg was still in the hotel's parking lot. It was only then that it dawned on me to call the reception at the Rodeway Inn and ask to speak to Vanessa Rumbaut. To my relief, the operator put me through:

" Hello," she answered tentatively. "Who is this?"

"Hi, Vanessa, I'm a friend of your mom's, and she told me about you flying to DC to help Marlon. I tried to meet your flight last night but missed you. Is Marlon with you? Are you guys ok?" I asked.

"Yes, yes, all is ok, and Marlon is fine. I just want to get him some breakfast and maybe buy him some new clothes."

"Well, don't go far, as we have already submitted a report to Homeland Security and Polaris, and they should have representatives there soon."

Greg alerted me at 11:30 a.m. about the arrival of Polaris and Department of Homeland Security agents.

"I can't believe it, Nancy! These agencies get millions of dollars, but the truth is, none of them are proactive first responders. And Polaris sending a young twenty-something girl into a potentially dangerous situation? It's unbelievable," Greg exploded on the phone.

Luckily, other than a sleepless night, the situation had a happy ending.

Marlon was placed away from his trafficker at "Youth for Tomorrow" in Bristol, Virginia, and enrolled in high school. He and Vanessa are best friends to this day.

EPILOGUE

Dave and I enjoying life together in El Salvador

When I was thinking about how to write the last chapter of this book, I realized I couldn't write a final chapter for this work. The work I've devoted my life to—helping the most vulnerable children—is certainly not done. In fact, the need remains and becomes greater as war, floods, earthquakes, and other natural and political disasters occur.

We adapted to Covid-19 in 2020 by adopting virtual missions for our members to visit via Zoom, connecting personally with our contact kids in Sierra Leone, Haiti, Nepal, Ecuador, and other countries. We were successful in fundraising for humanitarian projects, helping projects in Afghanistan, Haiti, Ecuador, El Salvador,

Peru, Philippines, Poland, South Africa and Ukraine. The concert AAI produced to help provide clean water for the Hopi and Navajo nations in the United States was a success.

Unfortunately, airports stopped commissioning human trafficking awareness training sessions in 2020 with the Covid scare and opted for the free Blue Lightning Training. It's good, but not nearly as impactful as an in-person training with real survivors. The silver lining is that because of our pioneering efforts and support from the flight attendant unions, human trafficking training is now mandated for flight crew in the US by the FAA Reauthorization Act of 2016, international guidelines with ICAO's Circular 352 in 2018, and private sector support through the International Air Transport Association, IATA.

Airline Ambassadors International is also making a difference by providing a way for flight attendants to escort children in need of medical care and a way for ordinary people to bring compassion into action though our humanitarian missions. That personal connection has truly changed the lives of the children we serve and the hearts of our members as well.

I led my last mission to our beloved El Salvador in January 2020. We had received a grant from Isagenix and were providing Wellness Training all over the world. Nayib Bukele had just become President, and one of his brothers had invited my husband, Dave, and I to come down and help the new dynamic President. I could not have been more thrilled, and since I can run AAI from anywhere in the world, we moved to El Salvador in March 2020. We rented a beautiful apartment in San Salvador for half of what we were paying in Washington for a one- bedroom.

Eventually we bought a lovely beach house in Barra de Santiago. It reminds me of Hawaii, but it's even more beautiful. This setting gives me plenty of time for deep contemplation, swimming, and long walks on the beach.

I would never have chosen the color scheme terracotta, golden yellow, and azure blue, but somehow it works. There are no walls, and the living room is outdoors, surrounded by hammocks and at least forty coconut palms in front of the blue Pacific. The sound of waves on the shore and dozens of melodious birds fill our audible senses. Dave and I walk the beach every night with our little york-ie, and on the way home, I raise my arms in prayer position to the golden light of the setting sun and silently send thanks to the Creator in the breeze. As the twilight sky fades from blue to peach to violet hues, we dip our bodies in the silky aqua water of our pool. Sometimes the full moon rises above the Palapa that shades our home, or pelicans fly over in perfect formation.

Dave's amazing efforts with the CASA program have been supported here by the Ministry of Housing, which he and Armando (Nayib's father) started so long ago. He accepted the position of Executive Director of the new Ministry of Design and Development, reporting directly to Nayib Bukele, President of El Salvador. I have never seen him so happy (although he still squeezes in mountain bike rides to the top of the volcano, 10 mile runs down the beach, and regular workouts). We have to pinch ourselves to realize we have everything we ever dreamed of and an amazing network of sincere friendships.

To make it even better, his original passion for animals and the environment came together, too. Sea turtles lay their eggs on the beach in front of our house. Reuben Navarro, our caretaker, has been gathering their eggs since he was a teenager.

What a joy when he knocked on our door to have us join him on the beach to see the huge mama turtle laying her eggs. She had returned to the exact beach she had been born on about thirty years before. Her shell was about two feet long, and she must have weighed 100 pounds. After she laid her many eggs, she sauntered back into the ocean, and we felt we had witnessed a miracle.

The really fun part is when the baby turtles hatch about forty-five days later. This always happens at dusk, to give the babies the best chance of survival as only one out of 1,000 will survive into adulthood. When the babies hear the waves, they instinctively begin walking towards the water. What a delight it was to see those little ones starting off on their grand adventure as the orange glow of the fading sun dipped behind the ocean.

In general, it seems women are more spiritual and emotional, while men are more physical and intellectual. Dave, my husband, is my complement. He is constantly changing and evolving. He always brings substance to my life and everything I do. Dave pushes me to exercise every day and eat well. I inspire him with my intuition, joy and love. Together, we are stronger than we are alone.

Now, we have the incredible privilege of building a mission larger than ourselves and supporting a global emerging leader with the potential of impacting not only the 6.5 million people in El Salvador but becoming a model that will eventually impact the entire world.

Blessed are we indeed to have found a way to make our dream real, and in the words of a song from the Sound of Music, that made me cry as a little girl, remembering a mission from beyond this world:

"Climb every mountain,
Ford every stream,
Follow every byway,
'till you find your Dream
A Dream that will take
All the Love you can Give
Every Day of your Life,
For as long as you Live"

I hope reading this book inspires you to make a positive difference in this world.

The AAI webpage, www.airlineamb.org, will remain available to you with contacts to help you plan trips that can include volunteering and making a positive difference in our projects. You may think that adding a few days of volunteering to your itinerary would not make a difference. It may seem that delivering a few T-shirts or giving an orphanage first aid items for the children is not a big deal—-but it certainly is for those receiving children. To quote Mother Teresa, it's not how much you give, but how much love you put into giving that really makes a difference.

OUR HEARTS
ARE SPEAKING

A great picture of Kelly Lee, Leela Hansen, Sharon Stein, Christina Andersen, Steve Ellis and me during an AAI mission in Peru

The work I've done has been so rewarding, and each one of our stories is so unique that there is no way I can cover all of them in this book, but I am so proud of each one of our medical escorts, and mission leaders, and participants who get to the heart of what being an airline ambassador is all about. Here are just a few more from our past newsletters:

Colleen Morey (after her AAI trip to Bogota, Columbia)

"Christmas came to life for me in the small orphanage in the foothills of Bogota, Colombia. I am humbled before you as I face the reality of the trip. To say that it was life changing only diminishes the essence of all it was; I had yet in my life to encounter children who had never seen or received presents. As I struggle with re-entry into my structured life of schedules, phone calls and meetings, I am faced with emotions that are firsts for me. I had thought we were going there to troubleshoot and fix. I learned we were there to love these precious little children and I realized they needed to give their love to us. That is all they longed to do. We were overcome by its purity; unconditional nature, its child filled with eagerness and candor and its completeness.

The crippled little hands that clutched in their clumsy way to our necks, clutched more so to our hearts and resurrected in me the spirit of this joyous season. Inside my heart is fresh new joy that has been given to me by the two, three, five and seven-year-old little ones who leapt into my arms on sight, clung to my hands and pulled at my arms on sight, clung to my hands and pulled at my arm with tears on their faces when the hour came for us to depart. It was not for anything we had done or brought to them, but rather, we were there for them to love. Who would have known that in the end, the true gift became ours?"

Penny Rambacher after her trip to deliver aid to Afghan refugees:

"When you travel to make a difference, you get back more than you receive. At night I would lie in my comfy warm bed, and remember the refugees, sleeping on the ground in a cold dusty tent. As I washed my face with pH balanced facial cleanser I remembered the gaunt, dirt caked faces of the children shivering in torn, thin rags. They have no soap and their skin looked more like elephant hide than the soft peach flesh of youth.

How could I ever complain again about anything, after seeing thousands living in a freezing desert, a place with not a shred of greenery, not a singing bird, not a laughing child. Thousands chose to live there to escape the war and killing.

Beyond the lessons of personal gratitude, I came back with a message for my fellow countrymen. The Afghan people are not all terrorists; they are terrorized. We need to feel compassion for the innocent children. We need to care, share and build peace and understanding. Guns and bombs do not end terrorism; they breed more hatred. Let us begin the task of building a world of sharing and goodwill for all people."

Susan Christian AA flight attendant after her first escort trip

"I took Moises from his home in San Pedro Sula, Honduras to Detroit for further work on his heart. We were met at the airport by SIX family members who were so excited and grateful and they invited me to stay the first night in their home. Moises' mother was gracious and couldn't feed me enough! There was a steady stream of friends, neighbors and cousins flowing in and out of the house, shaking my hand and (in many instances kissing and hugging me) and planting wet kisses on Moises--lots of tears too. I look forward to picking him up and returning him to his mother. They want me to stay with them again & show me the nearby Mayan ruins. This was truly a wonderful experience!

Leeanne Hansen (about her trip to the Philippines)

"I had the privilege, honor and thrill of coordinating our first humanitarian trip to the Philippines. 65 beautiful children greeted us with cheers, hugs, and flower leis. We laughed so much with the children and one another, and we grew to care about them and their home. It was a team effort of LOVE from the heart, and we knew it, and we came away with a renewed spirituality, a closer bond of friendship with each other and the new friends and knowing the little difference we had made in these precious lives. In the end we got back much more than we gave."

Mireille Hanna from about her mission to Chiapas Village in Mexico

Mireille Hanna expected it would be her last trip to a Chiapas Village in Mexico as the journey is so difficult. However, when she saw young Manuela holding a newborn baby and crying with hopelessness in her dirt floored shack, with her 4-year-old trying to comfort her, everything changed.

As Mireille took a warm shower that night and pulled soft covers around her, she could not get the scene out of her mind. Manuela's husband had been the only support for this family, and since he abandoned them, they would never know such comforts.

"This became a turning point for me," Mireille said, "I went grocery shopping, packed a bag of clothing for the children and went back there. I gave Manuela the groceries and clothes, and told her I would replace her dirt floor with cement. What a joy to see her smile through her tears. Needless to say, it would not be my last trip to her village, and there are many other huts needing cement floors. I hope the help of Airline Ambassadors will bring smiles to this Chiapas village again."

Sharrye Moore after delivery of TWO 40-foot containers to the Dominican Republic

"Each of these special angels are partners like pieces of a puzzle, and the end result is a beautiful picture with underprivileged children receiving the education and healthcare all children are entitled to. It shows me that with a great team, anything is possible."

Cindy Paulus about the JetBlue missions she led to El Salvador

"AAI has created an amazing opportunity for me, my fellow crew members and JetBlue Airways. Not only are we delivering love, but a relationship has been established between JetBlue and the country of El Salvador."

Ruth Matranga (after trip to Addis Ababa - medical escort

"The deepest gift I've ever received is to help these children … who will remember us for all of their lives."

Elaine Osborne after waiting three years to adopt Gabriella from El Salvador

"We had a connection from the first day I met her--it was love at first sight! For me, this is a dream come true! Gabby now has many new aunts and uncles in the Airline Ambassadors family who are also thrilled to welcome her home!"

After adopting Gabby, Elaine brought her on many missions. Bibiana and Orlando Velarde also adopted a little girl they met on an AAI Mission.

David Ayala (9 years old) & Peggy Shelley, after Elaine's trip to El Salvador

"This is the most fun I've had on vacation" and Peggy Shelley added "I can't remember when our family has spent such beautiful and quality time together."

Pam Maloof - about her escort of Demetri from Detroit to Antigua

"Of all the children I have escorted, Demetri was truly memorable! I met his foster family at the airport in Detroit, and as we went through security, one of the screeners recognized him from local TV coverage about his surgery. I explained that I was with Airline Ambassadors and taking him back to his family on the island of Antigua. We were instant celebrities, and Dimitri loved the attention. When we finally arrived after 3 long legs, his family was thrilled to see him so normal and healthy. It was quite a contrast to the little boy who had left them a few months earlier. As an Airline Ambassador, I am so proud of my American Airlines family … agents, flight attendants, and pilots who fuss over these children and make them feel so special. I could not do it without them."

ABOUT NANCY RIVARD

Nancy founded Airline Ambassadors International (AAI) to provide for orphans and vulnerable children in 1996 while working as a flight attendant for American Airlines. AAI is the only non-profit leveraging connections with the airline industry to facilitate humanitarian efforts, and is recognized by the US Congress and the United Nations.

Prompted by the sudden death of her father, Nancy left a career management track, returned to a position as a flight attendant, to begin a profound search for meaning. During extensive travel over the next seven years, she saw the glaring inequities between the developed and developing world, and potential for the travel industry to play a more fundamental role building sharing, understanding and goodwill between peoples and cultures.

Nancy was honored with multiple awards such as Woman of Peace Award (1999), Ambassador of Peace Award (2000),

President's Award for Lifetime Achievement (2006), President's Volunteer Service Award (2013), Global Woman of the Year at the Academy of Television Arts and Sciences, Ambassador of Peace Award at the London Travel Market (2013, 2014), the Perdita Huston Human Rights Award. In 2015, the Foundation for a Slavery Free World honored her with the Human Rights Hero Award ns in 2023 in El Salvador by Gente Ayudando Gente. Airline Ambassadors has been featured in 146 TV features, 394 print and 73 radio features since their inception.

Nancy has a Master's Degree in Public Administration from Southern Methodist University and is married to contractor and environmentalist, Dave Rivard. Nancy's dedication to Airline Ambassadors International is unwavering as she continues to lead the organization's humanitarian initiatives and raise awareness about human trafficking. Her passion inspires individuals to travel and make a meaningful difference.